CU00841169

Thanks

Before embarking on the journey through the pages of this book, I want to express sincere gratitude to all the extraordinary people who have made this project possible.
First and foremost, I would like to wholeheartedly thank my wife Veronique. Thank you for having the patience to endure my passion for Jack Russell Terriers and for supporting me always, despite the time and effort I have dedicated to this passion.
A heartfelt thank you also goes to all the friends who share the same passion for terriers and work with them. Thank you for the shared experiences and for enriching my journey in this fascinating world, and thanks to all the great terriers I have encountered along my path.
A special thank you goes to Daniele Comiotto, who kindly shared his incredible photos, providing extraordinary visual beauty to this book.
This project is the result of dedicated and passionate individuals, and I want to thank each of you for contributing to making this book a reality.

With gratitude,
Angelo

Introduction

Welcome to the world of working terriers, specifically the Jack Russell Terrier and the Parson Russell Terrier! In order to facilitate reading, we will use the term "Russell terrier" to identify both breeds in terms of character and personality.

This book offers an exciting journey through the hunting traditions of these brave and tireless terriers. We will explore the history and strong bond between man and his faithful hunting companion, without delving into technical topics that would require more space.

Hunting with terriers has a long history deeply rooted in the rural traditions of many cultures, requiring skill, intuition, and respect for nature. Terriers are special dogs, selected for their agility, determination, and ability to locate and capture prey. Despite their small size, they are formidable hunters thanks to their courage and distinguishing tenacity.

This book is a tribute to terriers and their unwavering efforts in the world of hunting. You will discover the foundations of strategies used by terrier experts, terriermen, exploring work like earthdog trials and the pursuit of foxes and other prey. Hunting for terriers is not just about practicality; it also demands a deep understanding of ethics and respect for animals and the surrounding environment.

Lastly, the book celebrates the extraordinary bond between man and his terrier, a partnership built on mutual trust. Whether you are experienced hunters or curious enthusiasts, this book will take you on a journey into the realm of terriers and their abilities.

Happy reading!

Index

The Origins of the Terrier

Terrier, it's curious how a term with a French-sounding and Latin-origin name can fully identify a working dog that had its complete development and recognition on English soil. But let's delve into where this type of dog comes from and its evolution in detail.

Ancient cave depictions bear witness to the collaboration between humans and dogs from the times when animals like cattle, sheep, and pigs were raised, and dogs played a crucial role in daily life. The various sizes of dogs were associated with different purposes such as territory defense, hunting, and protection from small nuisance animals. One of the many ancestors of our modern dogs was discovered at the Trana peat bog and was nicknamed the "peat bog dog".

Studies conducted by zoologists, paleontologists, and archaeologists have identified it as the first domesticated dog, also known as Canis familiaris palustris. This dog was employed for hunting small animals like rabbits and rats, as well as alerting humans to approaching danger. Its close collaboration and coexistence with humans, along with its favorable size, facilitated the development of its adaptability and hunting abilities.

Ancient cave paintings dating back to 5000 B.C. depict the possible ancestors of our current small-sized dogs, believed to originate from Central Africa, in the Congo region. From there, they spread and intermingled, eventually reaching our lands through North Africa.

In the book "Cynēgetikos", written around 400 B.C., Xenophon describes two varieties of hunting dogs: the beagle and the foxhound. While detailing the hunting techniques for hare and fox, he underscores the qualities required for a hunting dog:

V n'altra forte anchor de Cani eletti *Trouafi con fattezze altiere e belle.* *Quefti Caftori gia furono detti,* *Perche fue membra a fi fpedite e fnelle* *Diedero al gran Caftor dolci diletti,* *Pria che fplendeffe il Ciel fra l'altre ftelle.* *Quefti, con leggier corfo e prefto piede* *Fan di Lepre,e di Dame altiere prede.*	There is another type of chosen dogs, with a proud and beautiful appearance. Named Beagles as such, for the memory of the swift and sleek joys they gave to the great Beagle, before the sky shone among the stars. These, with speed and grace, make hares and foxes their own prey.
Portan la fua grandezza alteramente, *Con piccolo capo, e con uenofa fronte:* *Negr'han l'un e l'altro occhio rifplendente:* *Piccole orecchie, e giu pendenti, e pronte;* *Hanno ancho il petto largo & eminente:* *Li piedi inanzi corti, e fi confronte* *La spalla e'l petto, e'l tondo collo infieme,* *Longo e fottile in le parti supreme.*	They are proud, with a small head and veined forehead, they have shiny eyes of black color, ears are small, hanging and alert, they have a broad and significant chest, their front legs are short and turned forward, the shoulder, chest, and round neck are long and slender in the upper parts.

Di coste adorno il caffo, e'l uentre ftretto,	The torso is clearly visible and the abdomen tight,
Sarà piegato in foggia d'una naue.	resembling the keel of a ship,
Graffo il fuo lombo, e alquanto ritondetto,	the loin area is fatty and round,
Graffe le cofcie, e affai carnofe e caue.	thighs are big, fleshy, and hollow.
Longa la coda e'l piè dietro groffetto	With a long tail and stout hind leg,
Neruofo, e come al Ceruo anchor s'inchiaue,	nervous like a young deer,
E uagamente poi l'altezza auanzi	and of equal height both in stature
Da mezo indietro le parti dinanzi.	and in length.

From: "The Four Books of Hunting" (1556) by Tito Giovanni Scandianese. Page 65. (Giovanni Scandianese, in 1556, revisits and translates the works of Xenophon for the Fourth Duke of Ferrara.)

Scandianese's testimony confirms that the described dog is of small size, with proportional height and length, thus excluding the "dachshund" type and paving the way for other breeds known today as small sighthounds, which are ancestors of terriers.

Even in Rome, we find evidence of ancient hunting dogs in the writings of Ovid and Varro. Ovid explains how to obtain good puppies from the breeding females, while Varro provides advice on buying dogs, describing different canine types and their characteristics. Roman art in general has left us frescoes, sculptures, mosaics, and coins depicting dogs similar to our Cirneco, as well as pointing dogs and molossoids.

In ancient Rome, dogs were particularly beloved, to the extent that specialized officials called "procuratores cinogiae" were dispatched to the provinces of the empire to search for and select dogs of noble lineage. These dogs were then transported to Rome to be trained and used for breeding. The Romans classified dogs into various categories: "venatici" (hunting dogs), "pastorales" (herding dogs), and "villatici" (guard dogs for farms, houses, fields, and camps). Hunting dogs were further divided into "sagaces" (those who followed the tracks of game), "celeres" (those who chased it), and "pugnaces" (those who attacked it).

The important characteristics of hunting dogs are also described in the work "Cynegetica" (KYNHGETIKA or KUNHEGETIKA) by the Greek poet Oppian of Apamea, dating back to 300 A.D.

Oppian explains how small-sized dogs are particularly suitable for hunting game in the woods.

Ἔστι δέ τι σκυλάκων γένος ἄλκιμον ἰχνευτήρων,
βαιόν, ἀτὰρ μεγάλης ἀντάξιον ἔμμεν' ἀοιδῆς·
τοὺς τράφεν ἄγρια φῦλα Βρετανῶν αἰολονώτων·
αὐτὰρ ἐπικλήδην σφᾶς Ἀγασσαίους ὀνόμηναν.
τῶν ἤτοι μέγεθος μὲν ὁμοΐϊον οὐτιδανοῖσι
λίχνοις οἰκιδίοισι τραπεζήεσσι κύνεσσι,
γυρόν, ἀσαρκότατον, λασιότριχον, ὄμμασι νωθές,
ἀλλ' ὀνύχεσσι πόδας κεκορυθμένον ἀργαλέοισι
καὶ θαμινοῖς κυνόδουσιν ἀκαχμένον ἰοφόροισι·
ῥίνεσι δ' αὖτε μάλιστα πανέξοχός ἐστιν Ἀγασσεύς,
καὶ στιβίῃ πανάριστος· ἐπεὶ καὶ γαῖαν ἰόντων
ἴχνιον εὑρέμεναι μέγα δὴ σοφός, ἀλλὰ καὶ αὐτὴν
ἴδμων ἠερίην μάλα σημήνασθαι ἀϋτμήν.

There's a valorous breed of hunting dogs,
small yet so deserving of great praise for their intelligence,
bred by the wild tribes of the Britons,
improperly known by the name Agassei.
Their size resembles that of feeble and greedy domestic dogs,
But they are light, devoid of fat, with a curly tail, shrewd eyes,
and well-stretched legs with sharp claws, and they run swiftly, with
powerful breath.
Especially, Agasseus is highly skilled in using its nostrils,
and the most adept in running. Indeed, it's remarkably skilled at
finding tracks while hunting,
as well as discerning scents from the air as they are inhaled.

From: KINHGETIKON by Oppian, Book A (1813, Oppian's Kynegetika, page 15).

They are called "Agassaious", described as slim and small dogs, similar to hares, that hunt in the burrows they inhabit. They are bred in a way that a hand can encircle their body. They make great companions at home and take great joy in being guided for the hunt. Unfortunately, Oppian doesn't delve much into their morphology and color, but he confirms that their ancestors were highly skilled in the tasks assigned to them. These hunting dogs were bred by the wild groups of the Britons and were distinguished by their extraordinary ability to sniff and follow the tracks of animals, both on the ground and in the air.

The Greeks and Romans were aware of hunting dogs in general and bred them. Initially, hunting dogs were imported to Britannia by legionaries from Greece, but later they were exported to other regions as well. Oppian's accounts confirm this fact and demonstrate how the presence of small-sized hunting dogs was already widespread in Britannia in the first century A.D.

For further confirmation regarding small-sized burrowing dogs, we have to wait another 800 years, when in the Lex Baivvariorum, a breed of dogs that fits the sought-after characteristics is described:

TITVLVS XIX. *De canibus & eorum compofitione.*	CHAPTER 19. The Dog and Its Composition.
... *VI. De eo cane quem* **bibarhunt** *vocant, qui fub terra venatur, qui occiderit, alium fimilem reddat, & cum fex foldis componat.* ...	... 6. Of this dog they call bibarhunt*, which hunts underground and brings down prey of its own size, one can buy for six shillings. ... * Biber-hunt, Beaver-Hunt Dog

From: Corpus juris germanici antiqui ... Lex Baivvariorum pg. 320

The attribution of the value of "six shillings" to the dog bestowed even greater importance upon this small hunter, as it demonstrated that its value corresponded to its actual weight. It was a way to emphasize that the dog was worth exactly what it weighed.

Moving further in time, in works dating back to the 1400s, we can find a 14th-century engraving in Strutt's work "Sports and Pastimes", depicting a dog assisted by three men as it pushes a fox out of its burrow. From the engraving, we can't discern the dog's color or whether there's another dog inside the burrow that flushed out the fox. However, what is clear is that the dog has a slender body, resembling a small sighthound, with short fur and erect ears. Even more evident is the portrayal of the engraving itself, capturing an authentic moment of burrow hunting.

1347. The invasion of the Romans did not probably restrict the venatorial pursuits of the Britons, as history is silent as to any such enactments; neither would restrictions of this kind have been in unison with the general conduct of these invaders on such matters. But, as we have elsewhere noticed by introducing their amphitheatrical spectacles here it is probable the legitimate chase was feebly pursued, and consequently but little improved, under their domination. An old MS. recorded in Strutt, is illuminated with a representation of a party of hunters of those times in the act of unearthing a fox (fig. 203), whose bolting as we are told was not then noted by a view halloo, but by a sonorous blast from a cow horn; and the mort or death, without doubt, called forth poetic strains from some venerated bard, for even in these early times venation, music, and poetry, marched hand in hand. Can we therefore want any further proof of the high bearing of field sports when we find them so constantly in such company; the very deities in those times were all renowned sportsmen.

From: An encyclopaedia of rural sports:... (1870) by Delabere Pritchett Blaine page 380 part IV

After Strutt, Dr. Caius, upon Gesner's suggestion, was the first to write about English Dogs. With his work "De Canibus Britannicis", John Caius described and synthesized the profile of dogs present in the Anglo-Saxon territory, which eventually gave rise to the modern Terrier.

In his work, Caius closely examined the characteristics and distinctive traits of English dogs, providing a comprehensive overview of the various breeds and their peculiarities. He observed that these dogs were small and compact in size, with short and sturdy legs, and well-developed muscles. Their coat was rough and bristly, offering protection against weather and thorns during hunting expeditions.

Caius also highlighted the intelligence and liveliness of these dogs, which made them excellent in digging work and hunting foxes in burrows. He described their tenacity and courage, as well as their ability to follow tracks and catch the scent of game. These dogs were considered loyal and tireless companions, ready to follow their owner in hunting adventures.

Through his work, Caius contributed to spreading knowledge and appreciation of English dogs, laying the foundation for the subsequent evolution of the Terrier breed. His observations and detailed descriptions helped better understand the unique qualities of these dogs and recognize their significance in English hunting tradition.

Qui odoratu fatigat, & prompta alacritate in venando utitur, & incredibili ad investigandum sagacitate narium valet: a qua re nos sagacem hunc appellamus, quem Graeci ad investigando ἰχνεύτην (ἴχνος), à nare ρινηλάτην dicunt. Huic labra propensa sunt, & aures ad os usque pendulae, corporisque media magnitudohh.	That kind of dog which nature has endowed with a sophisticated sense of smell, whose property resides in the incredible wisdom of the nose and in hunting, to these we give the name of dogs with a keen sense of smell (Sagax), which the Greeks call -orma-, and the nose -explorer- (baldowern in German). The lips protrude, the ears hang down to the mouth, the body is of medium size.
*Sunt qui vulpem atque taxum solum, quos **Terrarios** vocamus; quid subeant terrae cuniculos, more viverrarum in venatu cuniculorum, & ita terrent mordentque vulpem atque taxum, ut vel in terra morsu lacerent, vel è specu in fugam aut casses cuniculorum ostiis inductas compellam. Sed hi in sagacium genere minimi sunt.*	These are the ones that only hunt foxes and badgers, which we call Terrarios; and which make the burrows of the earth their own, like the ferret in hunting, and by frightening the fox and the badger, as, for example, on the surface, its bite tears, so from a dark cave and hostile burrows, it lures the prey into a trap. But these are the smallest of the wise species.

From: De Canibus Britannicis (1576) by John Caius

The Saxons have left an indelible mark on England, a connection that still resonates today in the word "Hunde" (from modern German "hund", meaning hunting dog), which echoes among the hunting cognoscenti. Hunting was considered an art by the Saxons, and they had already developed distinctive characteristics in their dogs. Among these, we find the Terrare (Terrarius), the

Harier (Leverarius), and the Blub-hunde (Sanguinarius), all belonging to the Hunde (Sagax) type.

The reference to these sharp and small-sized dogs often echoes in literature, as in Rawdon B. Lee's book "A History and Description, with Reminiscences, of the Fox Terrier" (1889), which also quotes John Caius. These accounts underline the importance and ancient tradition of hunting dogs in English culture.

In the pages of this book, Lee explores the history and description of Fox Terriers, highlighting their unique qualities and the central role they played in fox hunting. Through his words, passion and admiration for these working dogs shine through, whose skill, intelligence, and determination made them extraordinary hunting companions.

The quotes of John Caius, a pioneer in studying English dogs, add a historical perspective and a connection to the ancient roots of this breed. His observations and descriptions testify to the presence of small-sized, sharp hunting dogs since the time of the Saxons, which have continued to evolve and contribute to the English hunting tradition over the centuries.

These testimonies, combined with the continued dedication and passion of hunting enthusiasts, have helped keep alive the legacy of English hunting dogs, including Fox Terriers. Even today, the presence of these dogs in hunting activities and their role as faithful companions pay homage to England's rich hunting history and the grand terrier tradition.

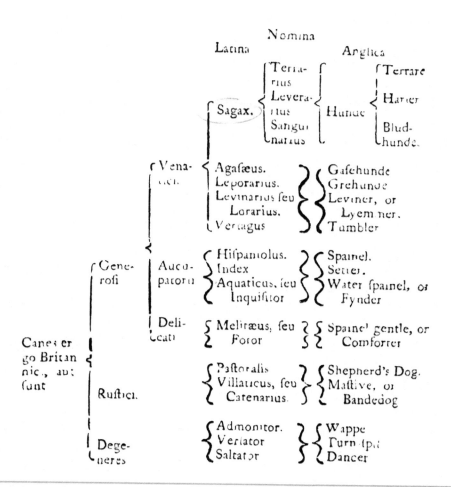

This is "of a dogge called terrar, in Latin Terrarius". Of him the old writer says, "Another sorte there is which hunteth the Fox and the Badger or Greye onely, whom we call Terrars, because they (after the manner and the costume of ferrets in searching for Connyes) creep into the grounde, and by that meanes make afrayde, nyppe and bite the Foxe and the Badger in such sorte that eyther they teare them in pieces with theyr teeth, beyng in the bosome of earth, or else hayle and pull them perforce out of theyr lurking angles, darke dangerous, and close caues;...

Also called Basset or Chien terrier, they were already referred to as terriers by Jean Nicot (1560-1600) in the

16th century. However, the translation by Turberville distorted the name into "terryer".

In René François's "Essay des merveilles de nature et des plus nobles artifices" (1626), the topic of the art of hunting is addressed, categorizing various types of dogs used for this purpose and briefly describing the morphological characteristics a good hunting dog should possess. Among these, a type of dog particularly suited for hunting foxes and badgers is mentioned.

Chasse du Renard, et Tesson *Les Chiens de terre qui se dient Basset & viennent de Flandre, entrent aux tasniers des Renards, & Tassons. S'ils y prennent quelque Tessonneau, il le faut faire tuer en la tranchée ou pertuis, à la maison leur faire curée du foye, &c. leur monstrant la teste de leur gibbier. Pour façonner les ieunes Chiens, on coupe la machoüere d'embas à un vieux Renard uif, où il a fes crochets & maistresses dents, laissant celles d'enhaut qui semblent terribles, & ne peuvent mordre; & lors les Chiens front rage.* *Les Renards sont leurs terriers en lieu, où l'on ne puisse bescher, & sentant les abbois bouclent & fortent aussi tost. Poui tournoyent long temps en leur païs deuant qu'en sortir. La curée en fait comme u Loup, ou sur sa peau y mettant les friandises.*	Fox and badger hunting Earth dogs called basset hounds, originating from Flanders, go into the dens of foxes and badgers. If they catch any badger, they must be killed in trenches or pits; at home, they should be skinned by fire, and so on, showing them the head of their trophy. To train young dogs, the jaw of an old dead fox is cut, leaving the upper ones that appear terrifying but cannot bite, and then the dogs become furious. Foxes have their dens in places where one cannot drink, and upon hearing the barking, they immediately close and fortify them. Then they roam in their territory for a long time before leaving it. The hunt is carried out as with a wolf, placing delicacies on its skin.

From: *Essay des merveilles de nature et des plus nobles artifices (1626) by René François*

This reference confirms the existence of dogs specifically selected for fox and badger hunting, emphasizing the attention dedicated to creating dog breeds specialized for certain prey. It is evident that even in those ancient times, fox and badger hunting required dogs with specific skills, capable of tracking and adapting to the needs of these particular targets.

The inclusion of such hunting dogs in the "Essay des merveilles de nature et des plus nobles artifices" highlights their importance in the realm of hunting and their reputation as faithful and capable companions for hunters. These dogs were deemed essential for hunting success and represented a fundamental component in the hunting culture of that era.

This historical testimony allows us to trace the origins of terriers specialized in fox and badger hunting, recognizing the value and significance they have held over the centuries. The dedication to selecting and refining dog breeds for specific hunting tasks speaks to the passion and competence of ancient hunters in creating dogs suitable for the demands of the hunt.

*Chien terrier: as Baffet; A **Terrier**.*
Earth dog: like a Basset; a Terrier.

From: A French and English dictionary (1673) by Randle Cotgrave

In 1699, in "The history of the works of learned, or an impartial account of books", what Caius had already summarized in his "De Canibis Britannici" is confirmed. However, in this new publication, different English nomenclatures are presented compared to those of Caius. The term "Terrare" is transformed into "Terrier-Hound", giving the breed a name with a more Anglo-Saxon sound. This linguistic choice probably reflected the evolution of the English language and the desire to give hunting dogs a designation that reflected their nature and British origin.

The introduction of the term "Terrier-Hound" might have also been motivated by the intention to emphasize the specific characteristics of these dogs, combining the term "Terrier" to indicate their specialization in working in burrows, and the term "Hound" to highlight their skill and use in hunting.

With the establishment of this new nomenclature, Terrier-Hounds gained even more recognition and popularity in the realm of hunting, becoming synonymous with skilled and reliable hunting dogs, particularly suited for burrow hunting and prey tracking.

The choice to adopt the term "Terrier-Hound" in the description of these dog breeds underscores the ongoing evolution of terminology related to hunting and demonstrates how the selection and specialization of dog breeds for specific tasks have been a constant in the history of hunting dog breeding in England.

Below, we find additional citations where the term "Terrier", over the years, is increasingly utilized in the Anglo-Saxon anthology.

"*The Fox being now earthed, the next Bufinefs is to get Shovels, Spades, Mattocks, Pickaxes, &c. to dig him out, if they think the Earth not too deep; and for the Eafe of themfelves, the Huntfman muft be provided with one or two* **Terriers***, to put into the Earth after him, to lay him up; that is, to fix him into an Angle, (which may be fooner done, according to the Opinion of fome, by putting a Collar or Bells round the* **Terrier's** *Neck) for the Earth oft-times confift of drivers Angles. The Ufe of this* **Terrier** *is to know where the Fox lieth; for as foon as he finds him, he contines baying or barking; fo that which Way the Noife is heard, that Way you must dig for him: And if he is dug up, he is fometimes thrown amongft the Hounds to blood and encourage them; ..."* ...

"*As concerning* **Terriers***, fome will have it that they are of a peculiar Species by themfeves; but however that be, it is certain that* **Terriers** *bred out of a Beagle and a Mungril Maftiff generally prove good; and indeed any fmall thick-fkinn'd Dog that hath Courage, and that will run into Holes, and lie baying at the Fox, is fit for the Purpofe; ..."*

From: The Complete family-piece; (1737) by C. Hitch page .296

"*The hound, the* **tarrier***, and fmall-fpotted fetting-dog, he confiders as of the fame family; and afferts, that they are often all produced at the fame litter, although the bitch fhould have been covered with only one kind of dog."* ...

"*We have feen above, that the maftiff, bull-dog, beagle, and hound, to which may be added the* **tarrier** *and fmall fetting-dog, are all produced in Britain from the fhepherd's dog tranfported from cold climates. ---"*

From: Observations on the means of exciting ... (1777) by James Anderson p.126,127

"*Of the two fort I prefer the rough, or wire-haired, being generally good shouldered Dogs, and well filleted. Smooth-haired Beagle are commonly deep hung, thick lipped, and large noftrilled, but often fo foft, folid, and bad quartered, as to be fhoulder-fhook and crippled the firft feafon's hunt, and have frequently that unpardonable fault of crook legs, like the* **Tarrier***, or right Bath Turnfpit."*

From: Cynegetica, or Essay of sporting (1788) W. Blane, W. Gomerville, F. Squire p.118

> *"But before they departed from these ugly earth-holes, an ill-contrived urchin, or a cur out of shape, and deform'd, (as they described hime), but we call him **Tarrier**, and they by the name of a **Whitwratch** (bastard-brood of the fox) as the servants apprehended; so might any man as well as they rationally conclude, as by the circumstances given us by their description."*

From: Northern memories, calculated for the meridian of Scotland (1821) Richard Frack p.161

The highly unusual name "Tarrier" originates from the old French term "Terrier" and the early medieval English words "Terrere" and "taryer". This nickname was occasionally given to individuals who cared for and trained the hunting dogs of Lords, tending to and instructing these skilled hunters.

Over time, the word used to describe these earth dogs underwent changes, but this was of minor importance compared to the remarkable intrinsic qualities of the animal.

The 19th century marks an important milestone in the selection of the Russell-type terrier. This Terrier, still known today as the Jack Russell Terrier or Parson Russell Terrier, is one of the most popular and well-known Terrier breeds in the world. Its origins are fascinating, although they are not entirely clear and unequivocally defined. It is said that the breed originated in the United Kingdom, thanks to the work and dedication of Reverend John Russell, from whom it takes its name. Reverend Russell was a passionate hunter and dog lover, particularly interested in fox hunting. John wanted a hunting dog capable of adapting to the specific needs of underground hunting and chasing foxes within burrows, but we will discuss this later.

What is certain is that dogs similar to terriers, with the same abilities, existed from ancient times, as evidenced by numerous writings that extol their prowess in underground work for fox hunting, badger hunting, otter hunting, or other small animals. However, the effective use of the Terrier required dogs of extremely small size, agility, and tenacity, a characteristic not possessed by all.

In the seventeenth century, the terrier was primarily employed for hunting rats and weasels that infested the English countryside. From this specific hunting requirement, the terrier breed with unique characteristics developed that made it one of the most skillful and suitable animals for this task. Its determination, agility, and tenacity continue to make it a hunting companion and a loyal friend to many hunting enthusiasts today.

Ratting

Despite fox hunting being universally recognized as the noblest sport in which terriers are employed, it should be noted that since ancient times, these dogs have been trained for another equally important task: hunting and killing rats in homes, farms, warehouses, and other structures. Their ability to dig and chase rats made them perfect for this crucial role. They were often used to protect food supplies and prevent the spread of diseases transmitted by rodents, which posed a threat to human and animal health.

Even today, despite numerous methods for managing rat infestations, many terrier owners continue to train and harness their incredible abilities to tackle this challenge. Terriers are tireless hunters, with unmatched determination in pursuing these pesky rodents.

Their speed, agility, and intuition make them true experts in locating and capturing rats. They can infiltrate even the narrowest corners and the most intricate burrows, following the scents and traces left by their small adversaries.

The importance of this terrier skill goes far beyond simply eliminating rats. These rodents can cause considerable damage to structures, harming materials and electrical wiring, compromising the integrity of constructions, and jeopardizing safety. Moreover, rats are carriers of dangerous diseases for humans, such as leptospirosis, salmonellosis, and the plague. The presence of a terrier trained to manage this threat helps ensure a healthier and safer environment for everyone.

Ratting, which involves capturing and killing a large number of rats, can sometimes be difficult to justify in terms of purpose. Rats are rodents from the Muridae family, of medium to large size, with an average weight of around 400 grams, but under favorable conditions, they can reach double that weight. These animals can produce up to 900 offspring per year and pose a serious threat.

Characterized by a rough coat with spiky hairs and a tail longer than their bodies, rats possess powerful jaws and a dental structure that allows them to sever and consume virtually anything in their path. Being omnivores, they disdain nothing and, before eating an unfamiliar food, they taste a tiny amount to ensure it won't harm them, then recognize it as food. These survival strategies enable rats to adapt even in hostile environments with limited resources available.

Throughout the centuries, terriers have been called by various names, but the term that most closely approximates the present-day definition is "Terrarios", meaning earth dog. Our canine ancestors have excelled over the centuries in hunting small animals, becoming infallible rat exterminators. Their speed, focus, quick reflexes, and jaw strength contribute to hunting and killing rats in large quantities.

In 19th-century England, the custom of using terriers in gambling competitions was prevalent. These challenges involved terriers of various breeds, pitted against each other to hunt and kill as many rats as possible within a set time limit. The competitions were highly popular, drawing numerous spectators who bet on the outcome of the challenges.

While this practice was primarily considered a form of gambling in the past, today many terrier owners continue to train them for rat hunting for practical purposes, such as pest control. In 19th-century London, Rat-bating reached its peak popularity, with competitions aimed at killing the most rats in the shortest time possible. This form of gambling was so widespread that dedicated gaming halls existed for these competitions, where spectators placed bets on the outcome. However, despite the approval of the Cruelty to Animals Act in 1835, this law only applied to larger animals, allowing underground meetings and illegal bets involving terriers.

Fortunately, the practice of Rat-bating declined in the early 20th century when owners were persecuted by law. Subsequently, during the World Wars, terriers played an essential role in the trenches, protecting soldiers from this small yet dangerous enemy. Their ability to hunt and eradicate rodents helped maintain clean environments

Catching a rat
(Parson Russell Terrier - Mambo's Alfie)

and safeguard the health of wounded soldiers by preventing disease spread. In this way, terriers demonstrated their significance in defending territories and ensuring the survival of our parents and ancestors.

In the trenches, our brave four-legged companions faced a small and cunning enemy, present in millions of specimens. Their proliferation in wet areas was immense, and the trenches were overrun by these creatures. Keeping those places clean was a challenging task as soldiers sought to defend the territory. It was difficult to imagine what those soldiers were experiencing in those moments. In addition to the human adversary, they also had to confront an enemy that devoured supplies and damaged equipment. The infirmaries and shelters had to be kept as clean as possible to prevent the spread of diseases among wounded soldiers, and the water, an essential element for survival, had to be drinkable and free from contaminants.

Even during the nighttime hours, soldiers had to contend with the presence of this stealthy, small, silent, swift, and hungry intruder. No one was safe, and wounds inflicted on soldiers while asleep constituted one of the main causes of epidemics.

This is why our valiant terriers were of great utility in defending the territory, hunting, and safeguarding the health and survival of the militia. Our small terrier friends demonstrated their courage, dedication, and value in extreme circumstances, earning a special place in the history and hearts of those who lived through those challenging times.

Terriers

Not all terriers in the English territory had the same characteristics simply because traveling was difficult, expensive, and slow. Each district tended to breed its own type of terrier. Some prioritized breeding for work, while others focused more on appearance. Selection criteria were not always consistent, and crossbreeding often occurred due to economic reasons, sometimes disregarding morphology and character.

Before the 1700s, white terriers were looked down upon and often excluded from breeding by English hunters due to suspicions of passing defects to offspring, particularly in the Northern areas. Testimonies suggest that a predominantly white bulldog selection led to genetic disorders and deafness. These defects could be attributed to close inbreeding, where frequent crossings of the same bloodlines result in a genetic impoverishment, amplifying defects. However, it's also true that from a selection of white Cairn Terriers, Major Malcom of Poltalloch managed to create the White West Highland Terrier, a dog with a white coat rarely seen in England before the 1800s.

Many sports were practiced by all inhabitants of the British soil, both cruel animal and human competitions. Often, the entertainment aspect prevailed over the actual danger and well-being of individuals. These sports could even be classified based on social classes, ranging from fox hunting, badger hunting, ratting, to dog fighting. The scenarios were often brutal, to the point where the thrill of sport and amusement overshadowed the dogs' well-being.

Selection was primarily based on the dogs' abilities and courage. One of the favorite sports was sending the terrier into the badger's den for a capture, after which the badger was released to make the terrier enter the den again, repeating the process multiple times. The winner was the one who flushed out the badger the most times in the shortest time. This spectacle was undoubtedly brutal for the dogs and not gratifying for the people of that era.

Another factor that altered appearance and structure was rat hunting, which gained prominence in 1720 when England was practically invaded by these small creatures. Rat extermination became a necessity for the inhabitants' health and evolved into a sport known as "the last sport of the poor". In the early contests, a hole of about ten square meters was dug, and around a dozen rats were placed inside. At the sound of the bell, the terrier had to kill them in the shortest time possible. However, the English Terrier was not created to be so brutal, so various breeders crossed it with the English Bulldog to obtain a breed better suited for rat hunting. It's worth noting that the 1800s Bulldog was quite different from the one we know today, not only in terms of morphology but also for its extremely aggressive character. You might wonder why they didn't directly use the Bulldog. Well, this breed was neither fast nor agile but had a strong bite and aggression. By combining the terrier's qualities with the Bulldog's, they obtained the ideal dog for rat hunting.

Thursday night, Oct. 24, at a quarter before eight o'clock, the lovers of rat-killing enjoyed a feast of delight in a prodigious raticide at the Cockpit, Westminster. The place was crowded. The famous dog Billy, of rat-killing notoriety, 26 lb. weight, was wagered, for twenty sovereigns, to kill one hundred rats in twelve minutes. The rats were turned out loose at once in a 12-feet square, and the floor whitened, so that the rats might be visible to all. The set-to began, and Billy exerted himself to the utmost. At four minutes and three quarters, as the hero's head was covered with gore, he was removed from the pit, and his chaps being washed, he lapped some water to cool his throat. Again he entered the arena, and in vain did the unfortunate victims labour to obtain security by climbing against the sides of the pit, or by crouching beneath the hero. By twos and threes they were caught, and soon their mangled corpses proved the valour of the victor. Some of the flying enemy, more valiant than the rest, endeavoured by seizing this Quinhus Flestrum of heroic dogs by the ears, to procure a respite, or to sell their life as dearly as possible; but his grand paw soon swept off the buzzers, and consigned them to their fate. At seven minutes and a quarter, or according to another watch, for there were two umpires and two watches, at seven minutes and seventeen seconds, the victor relinquished the glorious pursuit, for all his foes lay slaughtered on the ensanguined plain. Billy was then caressed and fondled by many; the dog is estimated by amateurs as a most dextrous animal; he is, unfortunately, what the French Monsieurs call borg-ne, that is, blind of an eye.-This precious organ was lost to him some time since by the intrepidity of an inimical rat, which as he had not seized it in a proper place, turned round on its murderer, and reprived him by one bite of the privilege of seeing with two eyes in future. The dog BILLY, of rat-killing notoriety, on the evening of the 13th instant, again exhibited his surprising dexterity; he was wagered to kill one hundred rats within twelve minutes; but six minutes and twenty five seconds only elapsed, when every rat lay stretched on the gory plain, without the least symptom of life appearing.' Billy was decorated with a silver collar, and a number of ribband bows, and was led off amidst the applauses of the persons assembled.

Billy, the rat killer - The sporting magazine, oct 1822:50

During this period, there was an uncontrollable increase in terriers and people who, for a fee, were responsible for exterminating rats in stables and houses. A breed called Cheshire Terrier, bred by John Tucker Edwardes and now extinct, was used to instill courage into the Sealyham Terrier.

The breeds were progressively mixed using strains of piebald and white bulldogs, eventually creating a line of dogs with white and piebald coats, which was primarily selected for courage. This also gave rise to the Bedlington and Dandie Dinmont Terrier breeds.

It was through these profound modifications that the bloodline developed, leading to the birth of the elegant Fox Terrier. According to writings, the Fox Terrier was developed through the crossbreeding of the "Old English White Terrier" and the "Black and Tan Terrier" with a rough coat. It was said that Reverend John Russell, disliking the bulldog blood, preferred a terrier with a more gentlemanly character.

The preference for this breed varied depending on the English regions. In the North, they favored dogs with a strong aggressiveness for burrowing hunting, while in the South, they preferred dogs capable of working together to catch foxes. More specifically, a dog that immediately bites its prey rarely barks and will be difficult to track underground.

However, there are also negative aspects, as a dog with bulldog blood will have difficulty stopping in front of a badger, but it will equally struggle to understand when it has made a mistake and is facing an adult badger.

> "... *Let Terriers small be bred, and taught to bay, when Foxes find an unsopt Badjers earthe, to Guide the Delevers, where to sink the Trench;*
>
> *peculiar is their breed, to some unknown, who choose a fighting biting Curr, who lyes and is sacre heard, but often kills the Fox;*
>
> *whit such a one, bid him a Beagle Join, the smallest kind, my Nymphis for Hare do use, that Crofs gives Nose, and wisdom to come in, when Foxes earth, and hounds all bayeing stand.*
>
> *This beagle blood, for this alone allow'd, reject it in the pack in every shape, the Ignorant, who oft have bred too high, do falsly think, the Nose thus to regain,*
>
> *the Crofs is wrong, it alters quite the breed, makes Fox hounds hang, and Chatter, ōre the Scent, as Vermin blood makes Beagles overrun, the Beagle, for the Hare alone desig'd,*
>
> *tho' Foxhounds some so falsly term, when small; if he marks well these hints, he cannot err."*

Records of the Old Charlton Hunt, The Earl of March (1910), pg.33

The crossbreeding that managed to enhance both scent and voice was precisely with bloodlines of the Beagle.

The alteration in morphology wasn't predominant, but the hunting instinct and intelligence prevailed in favor of the breed. With the emerging presence of the white color, it is thought more likely that this was the path of the ancestral Russell Terrier.

The Russell Terrier
(or Russell-type Terrier)

With the title of this chapter, the aim is to identify not only the Jack Russell Terrier but also the Parson Russell Terrier, whose origins are the same, although they have had different developments.

The story of Reverend John Russell is long and well-known to many, but for those approaching it for the first time, hearing it can be helpful in better understanding the kind of dog John was shaping.

He was born on December 21, 1795, at Belmont House, a residence located in the picturesque region of Devon. This period marked an era of revolutionary changes in various sectors, from agriculture to transportation, from population growth to technological and financial innovations. The Industrial Revolution was radically transforming the face of British society, opening new opportunities and presenting new challenges.

It was in this context of transformation that John Russell embarked on his journey to create a particular type of dog. Meanwhile, a significant event was taking place: the union between the Kingdom of Great Britain and the Kingdom of Ireland, which gave rise to the United Kingdom of Great Britain and Ireland. This historic event, known as the Act of Union, was a significant moment in British history and led to the creation of a broader union, symbolized to this day by the famous Union Flag.

John Russell's first mentor was his father, a well-known rector of Iddesleigh, a descendant of the Kingston Russell family branch that settled in Devonshire in 1551. He himself was a "Hunting Parson", and he taught his children

and pupils "the sport" from a young age. From him, John not only learned the basics of Greek and Latin but also what was then called "the noble science" (of hunting). "Work and play", that was his father's motto, and to instill this principle, he got a pony specifically for the boy's benefit. Upon achieving the highest grades, he rewarded him with sole possession during hunting days. For young John, no incentive was more effective, so he continued to study diligently.

From then on, his life was filled with commitments, from university to his ecclesiastical life, but in his free time, he always practiced his preferred "sport". Initially with ferrets and then with skilled hunting dogs, until in May 1818 (this is the presumed date), while walking toward Marston, he encountered a milkman with a marvelous terrier specimen: "Firstly, the color is white with only a dark brown spot on each eye and ear, while a spot no larger than a penny marks the base of the tail. The coat is thick, dense, and robust, designed to protect the body from water and cold, but it has no relation to the long rough coat of a Scottish terrier (it is believed to have had a Broken coat type). The legs are as straight as arrows, and the feet are perfect; the hips and the entire structure indicate courage and endurance, while the size and height of the animal can be compared to those of a female fox".

He made her his own and named her "Trump", becoming the progenitor of that famous breed of dogs that is still associated with the Russell type today.

The "Sporting Parson" (John Russell), also known as "Jack", continued his journey in his preferred sport, fox hunting, with the nobles of the time, who owned the finest dogs in the counties.

Mr. John Morth Woolcombe, Mr. Harris, Earl Fortescue, the Earl of Portsmouth, George Lane-Fox, and Henry Villebois were some of his companions in hunting.

Continuous incentives, the selection of dogs capable of cornering a fox in its den and intelligent enough to manage themselves better, held significant value for the sport he loved. He favored a dog that wouldn't just resolve the work within the den but could trap the cunning opponent as long as possible. In that era, there was a great extermination of foxes, either due to hunting or because farmers were tired of having their produce taken away, and for this reason, the sport had to be managed, in some cases, differently. The skill of John's dogs became necessary.

By the way, we recall a passage from his memoirs that reads: "Firstly, the color is white with only a dark brown spot above each eye and ear, while a similar spot, no bigger than a penny, marks the base of the tail. The coat, which is dense, thick, and slightly rough, is well-suited to protect the body from dampness and cold, but it has nothing in common with the long rough coat of a Scottish terrier. The legs are straight as arrows, the feet perfect, the loins, and the conformation of the whole-body indicative of strength and endurance, while the size and height of the animal can be compared to those of a female fox".

"I rarely or never see a true fox terrier nowadays", Russell recently said to a friend who was inspecting a dog show containing a hundred and fifty specimens with that designation. They've mixed so much different blood with the true specimen that, if he hadn't been told, he would have even confused Professor Bell himself trying to figure out which breed the so-called fox terrier belongs to.

"And how is it done?" asked the friend, eager to benefit from Russell's extensive experience in the matter. "Well, I remember the terriers of Rubie and Tom French of Dartmoor, and I also had some of the sort that were worth their weight in gold. They were true terriers, but certainly different from today's show dogs, as much as a wild rose differs from a garden rose. But the process", Russell replied, "is simply as follows: they start with a smooth-coated terrier bitch, then to achieve a finer coat, they choose an Italian Greyhound as a mate. The resulting puppy's ears are a concern for connoisseurs, so they turn to a beagle, and thus the unappealing defect is minimized in the next generation. Finally, to complete the mix, the intervention of a bulldog is required to provide the necessary courage, and the animals thus developed become, after careful selection, the fathers and mothers of modern fox terriers.

This version of their origins", he continued, "I have received from a well-qualified man to speak on the subject. It is true that bulldog blood imparts courage to the so-called terrier; it is unbeatable in killing any number of rats in a given period, it will fight against any dog of its own weight in a Westminster pit, it will pull out a heavier badger from a sett, and tear apart a tomcat, even possessing ten lives, before the poor tom can emit a lament. However, the fierceness of that blood is actually ill-suited, indeed fatal, for fox hunting, as a terrier that goes underground and grips onto its fox, as one so bred would, is much more inclined to spoil the sport than promote it. It enters to kill, not to make the animal it's attacking escape. Moreover, animals of this kind, if more than one enters a fox's den, are too inclined to forget the prey and fight amongst themselves; the death of one is occasionally the result of such clashes. Therefore, Russell had reason to be proud of the pure genealogy that he had possessed for so long and carefully guarded".

Russell didn't just have a passion for fox hunting, a sport practiced for most of his life, but he also had it for deer hunting, that ancient "sport of kings" which he often engaged in with his extensive experience.

He died at the rectory of Black Torrington on April 28, 1883, in his eighty-eighth year. He was buried in Swymbridge on May 3rd, and a thousand people attended his funeral.

His experience as a huntsman, rider, and judge of dogs speaks volumes about his life, divided between the church and sport, people and animals.

The Russell Terrier type is still present today with its keen, vigilant, intelligent, tireless, and fearless character.

The origin of its selection disappeared with him, and after his death, different paths were pursued to arrive at the type of dog we know today; one type that prefers taller dogs (Parson Russell Terrier), capable of running faster, and the other type (Jack Russell Terrier), smaller in stature and more agile underground. While the Parson Russell Terrier has an ideal shoulder height of about 33 cm for females and 36 cm for males, and a weight of 6-7 kg, the Jack Russell Terrier is slightly smaller, with a height of about 25-30 cm and a weight of 5-6 kg.

The functional morphological features in a Russell Terrier are the result of careful and targeted selection, and these characteristics have been developed to make the dog an excellent hunter.

Some of the main morphological features that contribute to the hunting capabilities of this breed are size and structure. The Russell Terrier is a small-sized dog, yet well-built and muscular. This compact and sleek structure enables them to move agilely and swiftly in tight burrows and underground spaces where prey often seek refuge.

Strong and powerful bite, allowing them to defend themselves or capture and kill prey effectively, even in challenging conditions or confined spaces.

Sensitive nose and highly developed sense of smell, aiding them in detecting the scent trails of animals underground. This ability is crucial for tracking and flushing them out from their hiding places.

Endurance, tenacity, and determination. When it comes to hunting prey, the Russell Terrier doesn't give up easily, continuing to work with tireless perseverance until it reaches its goal.

Digging ability. Their paws need to be strong and powerful. Their instinct to dig makes them perfect for hunting subterranean animals like foxes and badgers.

Agility and speed. This breed is incredibly agile and fast, qualities that allow them to chase and capture prey attempting to escape their reach.

In addition to the main functionalities, one of the most important characteristics for a Russell Terrier (both Jack and Parson) is the size of the chest, as it determines whether it will be able to pursue its prey underground. If the chest is too large, the terrier will be ill-suited for underground work, as it won't be able to navigate the tight spaces encountered in fox hunting. Even though foxes might appear to be larger animals, their bone

Spanning a terrier
(Jack Russell Terrier - M.B. New Angel for Chakys Jack)

35

structure is thinner compared to that of terriers, and their coat is dense and close-fitting, which gives them greater flexibility.

To assess the chest size, a measurement known as "spanning" is performed, which involves measuring the circumference of the chest. Using both hands, touching index to index and thumb to thumb, a circle is formed that represents the measurement of the span. Some individuals might not be able to connect the two thumbs and cover the entire circumference, while in other measurements, they might slightly overlap. It's important to take into account your own "plus or minus factor" and try to estimate a circumference of about 17 inches (approximately 43 cm), which corresponds to the ideal chest size in a terrier with a height ranging from 12 to 14 inches (approximately 30-35 cm). An adequately sized chest allows the dog to have enough room for the heart and lungs, ensuring the necessary flexibility for pursuing prey in underground work. The shape of the chest should resemble that of an egg in profile, with the wider end facing upwards, to allow free movement of the front legs. A chest that is too large could lead to widening of the elbows and compromise the dog's mobility. Therefore, it's important for the chest to have the correct size not only from a functional standpoint but also to ensure aesthetic balance.

When performing a span on a terrier, it's crucial to approach the dog calmly so that it's aware of being handled. Avoid sudden movements and do not grip the terrier tightly. With the dog on the ground or on a stable surface, gently lift the front legs and place your hands behind the elbows, around the chest. It's essential not to

lift the terrier excessively off the ground to prevent causing stress and tension.

Spanning is a useful tool for evaluating a terrier's chest, but it's not the only factor to consider in assessing a working dog. Nevertheless, achieving the ideal span is an important goal for the Russell Terrier, as it contributes to both its functionality and aesthetic appearance.

Another crucial aspect in the Russell Terrier is its barking. In addition to entering burrows, the dog must bark to allow the hunter to locate it. The bark and its tone hold particular importance, not only for frightening and cornering the prey but especially for the success of the hunt. The bark should be powerful, full, and never excessive; its tone should be audible at a distance of fifty meters, starting from low (even with a growl) and rising without interruptions to a medium pitch, with punctuated pauses, to indicate confidence and readiness to react.

In addition to barking, the tail covered an important characteristic of terriers. This tail is large at the base, robust, and serves a significant function. It was developed with its use in mind to pull the dog out of a burrow, thus its sturdiness was essential. However, in the past, the tail was often docked to prevent it from becoming an easy grip for the fox during the struggle in the burrow or to avoid the dog getting injured among brambles or roots. When docked, the tail took on the shape of a broom handle, and its length was approximately a little more than the width of a hand.

In the Russell Terrier, the coat holds significant importance, especially for long-haired dogs. The long hair provides a less firm grip for wild animals, consequently reducing the injuries the dog might sustain during the hunt. This is particularly advantageous when dealing with prey like the fox, which can be aggressive and combative.

Furthermore, the color of the coat plays a crucial role in identifying both the dog and the prey. The white coat of the Russell Terrier stands out from a distance and even when soiled with dirt and mud, it always presents a noticeable difference compared to the fox's fur. This distinctive color allows the hunter to easily identify the target of the hunt and to keep track of the dog's position during the pursuit.

The visibility of the white coat is particularly useful when hunting in wooded or dense terrains, where vegetation can make it challenging to spot both the dog and the prey. Without diminishing the importance of physical characteristics, the character and determination for the work performed are of vital importance in a Russell Terrier, which we will have the opportunity to discuss in the following chapters.

All these morphological features have led to different selections for a breed whose origins can nonetheless boast great temperaments. On one side, there are English clubs yielding to Australian clubs in favor of developing the smaller breed, and on the other side, English clubs favor the development of the "original".
Today, the two breeds are distinctly identified as Jack Russell Terrier and Parson Russell Terrier, although in their origin's history, the name changed frequently, causing not a few problems. This origin always managed to combine the working terrier that we know today.

Working Terrier

The concept of the "working terrier" represents a significant figure in the context of hunting dogs. This term, dating back to around 1400, describes the small utility dogs that follow prey inside burrows. Before the birth of the Russell Terrier, it encompassed all those small-sized dogs that displayed common qualities in their work.

"Working terriers" are known to be highly active, fearless, intelligent, reliable, and tireless. These fundamental characteristics make them excellent in their role as working dogs. Unlike conformation championships, where outward appearance and morphology are judged according to predefined standards, in the hunting context, greater importance is placed on the temperament and qualities that make a "terrier" a true working dog, capable of adapting to the task for which it has been selected.

In the hunting field, some working trials allow evaluating whether a dog has a more or less evident predisposition and whether it is suited for work in burrows. These trials highlight the hunter's nature and the dog's ability to perform its task effectively. It's interesting to note that, within the same breed, one dog can be morphologically beautiful but fearful, while another dog with various morphological imperfections can excel at adapting to the required work.

I'll never tire of saying it, but the primary physical characteristic that a working dog in a burrow, or working terrier, must possess is the size and shape of the chest, as these determine the type of prey the dog can hunt and the type of burrow it can enter. The fundamental rule is that the dog's chest size should be smaller than the burrow's

size. This allows the dog to focus on pursuing the prey without expending energy to widen the hole and without exposing its legs and muzzle to potential attacks.

A burrowing dog with a good chest is more agile and can breathe better in an environment with low oxygen. A dog with a bulky or barrel-shaped chest would have significant difficulties squeezing into or out of a burrow and would be clumsy in movements, and certainly wouldn't have a long life underground.

The dog's structure and build also play a fundamental role; consider the hind limbs, where correct angles allow greater propulsion in the burrow. Furthermore, this characteristic facilitates the dog's ability to move in the burrow and pursue prey with agility.

It's important to consider that I cannot expect an Airedale Terrier to fit into a rabbit burrow, just as I cannot expect a tiny terrier to chase a fox three times its size and weight. The hunting use of the dog must align with the selection that has been made.

From all this, one can understand the importance of both the temperamental and morphological aspects in working terriers. The dog must have the right physical and temperamental characteristics to perform its role effectively. Patterdale and Russell Terriers belong today to the category of "working terriers", also known as Fell terriers.

This category of terriers was originally trained and utilized to capture wild animals like foxes in the mountainous territories of the United Kingdom. These terriers are known to be brave, tenacious, and skilled in tracking and capturing their prey.

However, not everyone is aware that the primary criterion of a working dog is to have an owner who puts it to work. A working terrier isn't so by virtue of its birth or breeding assumptions, but rather due to the training it receives and its predisposition to hunting.

In the 1960s, hunting events increased in popularity, and the Russell Terrier found its place, eventually leading to the establishment of the future standard for its morphology and character. From the early dogs, which were unattractive in appearance, born from crosses of various breeds to enhance desired traits (straight forehead, narrow chest, and suitable neck length), excellent individuals began to emerge, sometimes crossed with Border and Lakeland terriers.

In the North, there were crosses with Fox Terriers that resulted in finer types, well-structured with straight legs but weaker jaws due to finer bones. Some breeders primarily aimed to improve hunting qualities, leading to the noticeable influence of the beagle.

Today, such crosses are frowned upon, but this is one of the many paths that the current Jack and Parson Russell Terrier DNA can take.

With the establishment of the Jack Russell Club of Great Britain (1960), these crosses faced challenges. However, even today, influences from these crosses or marked flaws in our companions can still be seen. The role of the Jack Russell Club of Great Britain played a significant role in the breed's character selection. Its founder, Mrs. Romayne Moore, was a great advocate for the breed. Coming from the Midland Working Terrier Club, of which she was the founder, and whose purpose was to select working terriers of various breeds, she managed to bring many important insights to the Club until she had to move abroad in 1960. During the decade when she was away from the club, no one managed to lead the club she formed with the same enthusiasm and competence, and the main qualities to support it were lost, both due to the successors' lack of enthusiasm and internal issues. Upon her return in 1970, she formed the Jack Russell Owners' Club, explicitly asking them to suggest a formal standard for the Jack Russell. The responses she received were nothing extraordinary until 1975 when a limited number of people formed the Jack Russell Terrier Club of Great Britain.

David Brian Plummer was elected president of the association, and with the help of Mrs. Moore, the first standard for the Jack Russell Terrier was designed, from which a register was created for all dogs that met this standard. There was a main registry and an advanced one. The advanced registry mainly consisted of male dogs that exhibited characteristics of uniformity, aiming to better define the breed's future.

The standard was as follows:

The Jack Russell Terrier Club of Great Britain

Objectives: The Central Committee has formulated the standard to achieve a uniform type of Jack Russell Terrier; and through conventions, teachings, discussions, and the formation of branches in all counties, to educate breeders and the general public about the correct type.

PROVISIONAL STANDARD, drafted in January 1975
Height: To allow for different sizes of Jack Russell Terrier, two heights are permissible: up to 15 inches above the shoulders; and 11 inches and more at the shoulder, to allow for the small-sized type.
Head: Head of strong bone structure with powerful jaw and well-developed cheek muscles. Dark almond-shaped eyes with well-pigmented rims and good nose pigmentation. Small V-shaped drop ears carried close to the head. (When viewed from the front, the fold of the ears will be slightly above the crown of the skull).

Teeth: The upper incisors' tips should slightly overlap the lower ones.

Body: Straight back, with a high-set tail, at least 4 inches in length, carried jauntily. The front of the body must be well-muscled with strong shoulders over straight front legs. The chest should be spannable with two hands behind the shoulders. The hindquarters should be well put together, with strong muscles and good angulation. Cat-like feet with unsightly hocks removed.

Coat: Smooth or broken (not long and woolly).

Color: Predominantly white, with light brown (tan), tricolored, or traditionally spotted (hound), including ticked or marked.

Undesirable Traits (any of these traits will render the terrier ineligible for the Advanced Register): Traits of other breeds, such as Sealyham, bull terrier, wire fox terrier, Lakelands, etc., pricked ears, crooked front legs, brindle coat, snipy nose, depigmented eye rims, curly tail.

Registration: All terriers belonging to club members can be registered in the Base Register. However, if an owner considers their dog or bitch of sufficient merit, they may present it to one of the regional inspectors for personal examination; if the inspector deems the animal of sufficient merit to continue the breed, and it does not exhibit hereditary signs of defects, the dog will enter the Advanced Register.

Note: Terriers must be at least 15 months old and registered in the Base Register, as described.

The history of clubs dedicated to the Parson Russell Terrier is rich in passion and commitment from breeders and enthusiasts alike. These clubs have played a fundamental role in the recognition and promotion of the Parson Russell Terrier as a distinct and valuable breed.

One of the most well-known clubs is the Parson Russell Terrier Club, founded in the United Kingdom in 1990. This club has been dedicated to preserving and promoting the breed, establishing breed standards, and organizing events such as dog shows and working trials to showcase the qualities of Parson Russell Terriers. The Parson Russell Terrier Club has also played a significant role in creating guidelines for responsible breeding and advocating for the interests of the breed.

In addition to the United Kingdom, there are also clubs dedicated to the Parson Russell Terrier in several other countries, such as the Parson Russell Terrier Association of America and the Parson Russell Terrier Club of Canada. These local clubs have contributed to the spread and promotion of the breed in their respective regions, working to preserve the distinctive characteristics of the Parson Russell Terrier and promote responsible breeding practices.

Through the collaboration and efforts of Parson Russell Terrier and Jack Russell Terrier clubs worldwide, the breed has gained a solid base of supporters and increasing recognition. The clubs continue to play a vital role in maintaining the integrity and health of the breed, as well as providing an important community and resources for enthusiasts.

Despite specific differences in appearance and conformation, both breeds share a set of distinctive characteristics that make them true terriers. Both types are small, energetic, bold, and full of life. They possess a lively personality, keen intelligence, and great determination in work and play.

Both breeds maintain a strong hunting instinct and a great desire to chase and confront prey. Their initiative and vitality make them excellent companions for active and dynamic individuals. They are also extremely intelligent and responsive, which facilitates their training and ability to learn new commands and tasks.

Despite the specific differences between the two breeds, such as size and certain morphological features, the character and fundamental qualities that define a terrier are common to both. Both the Parson Russell Terrier and the Jack Russell Terrier carry on the legacy of dedicated working dogs bred for hunting.

Fox Hunting

Fox hunting in England has a long tradition, attributed to an English nobleman of the eighteenth century. After an unsuccessful deer hunting expedition, the nobleman encountered a fox and, after a frenzied chase through woods, obstacles, jumps, and fords, he couldn't capture the cunning animal, despite the support of his hounds. This experience pleased the nobleman and marked the beginning of a tradition that lasted over 200 years.

Fox hunting in the nineteenth century was a widespread practice involving both the aristocratic elite and the working class. It was considered a prestigious sport reserved for those who could afford hunting horses, proper equipment, and access to private lands. Fox hunting provided an opportunity to socialize, demonstrate skills, compete on an equal footing, and enjoy nature and the company of fellow hunters.

Throughout the 1800s, fox hunting became increasingly organized and regulated. Hunting clubs and associations were established to organize hunting expeditions, set rules, and maintain order during outings. Hunters were required to adhere to a code of conduct that included respecting private property, ensuring the safety of other hunters, and treating the animals involved ethically.

Fox hunting required a good knowledge of the terrain and fox habits. Hunters needed to be able to identify tracks and clues left by the fox, as well as understand the behavior of the pack of Foxhounds in following the scent and finding the prey. The ability to navigate through various terrains, such as fields, woods, hedges, and watercourses, was essential for tracking the fox during the chase.

Foxhounds were the preferred hunting dogs for this type of hunt. These dogs were selected for their ability to track the scent of the fox and keep it in sight during the pursuit. They worked in groups, led by the "Master of Foxhounds", who managed and controlled them during the hunt. They were highly regarded and carefully handled, as they were crucial to the success of the hunting expedition.

During fox hunting, hunters used sound signals, such as horns and trumpets, to communicate with each other and coordinate the actions of the Foxhound group.

These signals had various meanings, such as announcing the sighting of the fox, indicating an ongoing chase, or

Pack of Foxhounds

signaling the capture of the prey. The sounds of the horns resonated across the countryside, adding an exhilarating atmosphere to the hunting experience.

Despite its popularity, fox hunting was also the subject of controversy and criticism. Some viewed hunting as an act of cruelty towards animals, while others were concerned about the damage caused to private property or the accidents that could occur during hunting expeditions. These concerns led to a debate on the ethics of fox hunting and the emergence of animal protection movements that sought to limit the practice or introduce stricter rules.

The fox hunting of that period reflected the cultural and social traditions of the time. It helped solidify rural and aristocratic identities, offering a way to connect with nature, demonstrate skills, and enjoy the company of fellow hunters. Despite criticism and subsequent regulatory changes, fox hunting left an indelible mark on the history of hunting activities.

The main element of the hunting action was the pursuit of the prey across the territory. Horseback hunters moved swiftly, following the pack of Foxhounds as they tracked the scent of the fox. It was a demanding activity that required physical endurance and equestrian skill. Hunters had to navigate varied terrain, overcome natural obstacles like hedges and ditches, and maintain focus during the pursuit. This demanded excellent orientation abilities and deep knowledge of the hunting grounds.

An important aspect of the hunting activity was the strategy of leading the fox towards an open area where mounted hunters could have better visibility and ease of movement. Foxhounds, trained specifically for this type of

hunt, worked in a coordinated manner to guide the fox to the desired location.

During hunting expeditions, it was common for the fox to seek refuge inside a den, interrupting the pursuit. Since Foxhounds weren't suited for underground hunting, smaller dogs like the Russell Terrier were employed for this purpose. The Russell Terrier was selected for its ability to flush out the fox without killing it. However, it's worth mentioning that the Russell Terrier wasn't the only terrier used for underground hunting.

When the Master, responsible for the hunting expedition, sounded the horn, the terrierman, an essential figure for fox hunting, would bring the dog to the den's entrance. Holding the dog by its tail, before releasing it, the terrierman ensured the terrier had the right determination to enter. Once released, the Russell Terrier would immediately start searching for the fox. If it managed to locate the fox and corner it with no chance of escape, it would start barking persistently. The Russell Terrier's barking had to be continuous, clear, rhythmic, and should never cease until the fox was retrieved. These characteristics were crucial because, being underground, the dog needed to make its voice heard by the terrierman who managed the hunting operation.

In the modern era of fox hunting, the dog's retrieval is facilitated by the use of radio collars that provide accurate positioning of the dog underground. However, in the past, reliance was placed on human hearing. Therefore, it was important for the dog to emit a constant and audible bark. Once the positions of the fox and the dog were identified and if they were unable to come out, digging would commence to retrieve both of them. The digging process required precise techniques, as any mistake could lead to the collapse of the tunnel and endanger the lives of the two animals. A square was drawn using a digging spade, and vertical digging was done while keeping the excavation walls straight to avoid an funnel collapse. Subsequent digs were made, each smaller in size, until the tunnel was breached. To prevent harm to the animals, the shovel was used as a divider between them. The terrierman could then retrieve the dog, and sometimes, the fox would be released afterward.

When the fox was captured, the moment was often celebrated with joy and satisfaction. It was a tradition for the hunters to gather around the prey and congratulate each other on the success of the hunt. Some hunters might also take a moment to admire the beauty of the animal and appreciate its strength and agility.

Fox hunting in the 19th century was more than just a sport. It was a social experience that involved a community of hunters, their horses, and hunting dogs. The hunters knew and supported each other, and often fox hunting was followed by parties and banquets to celebrate the event. It was a way to bring people together through a shared passion and forge lasting friendships.

Many things have changed over time, including the abolition of fox hunting as it was once practiced in England. Today, fox hunting is considered a "sporting pursuit", and the objective is no longer to kill the fox but to chase it.

The 19th-century fox hunting is remembered as an important part of hunting history, reflecting the cultural and social traditions of the era. While the practice itself has changed over time, the allure and energy of the fox chase continue to captivate and inspire hunting enthusiasts of all ages.

Digging

As the terrier traps the fox underground, preventing it from finding an escape route, the terrierman must be careful to accurately pinpoint the starting point for digging to retrieve both the terrier and the fox from the den. Before digging, it's important to pause and ask: Am I really sure the fox is cornered? Sometimes, one might start digging too early, only to discover that both animals have moved, perhaps to another tunnel farther and deeper. Before commencing the excavation, it's crucial to ensure that there's no chance of the fox exiting through other tunnels and that it's in a dead end.

Digging tools

The size of the excavation depends on the depth of the den, but generally, the hole should be large enough for the terrierman to work within it, yet not so big that it causes the walls to collapse. In terms of depth, a fox den can vary from a few centimeters to several meters below ground level, depending on the ground conditions and the chamber in which the fox has taken refuge.

During the digging operation, precise techniques are employed to prevent the earth from collapsing inside the tunnel, which could endanger the lives of both the dog and the fox. The process begins by marking out a square on the ground, and then two vertical holes are excavated, taking particular care to keep the tunnel walls straight to prevent funneling.

Digging with the terrier still in the ground.
(Parson Russell Terrier - Dido del Gatol)

It's normal for the terrier and the fox to shift slightly forward in the tunnel as soon as the surface is broken. This doesn't indicate that the dog is moving backward, but rather that it's continuing to advance, often overcoming a bend where it was blocked by the fox's sharp teeth. In fact, many foxes are skilled at defending themselves effectively in tight and curved tunnels.

Typically, the process starts with an access pit that has a square or rectangular shape, with a width of about 1.5-2 meters and a depth of around 1 meter. Once the access pit is created, terriermen start digging the entrances that lead to the fox's den. These tunnels can vary in length, depending on the distance between the access pit and the fox's den, and they're constructed using a combination of shovels and other digging tools.

Several specific tools are used for the excavation, including a narrow and sharp-bladed shovel that allows precise and easy cutting of the soil. Additionally, buckets or baskets are used to remove the excavated soil.

Once the soil is carefully removed and if the terrier and the fox are spotted, a shovel is usually used as a barrier between the two animals to prevent them from injuring each other. This way, the terrierman can safely retrieve the dog and capture or release the fox if necessary to continue the hunting pursuit.

Knowing that your Russell Terrier is underground and relies on you to catch the fox leads to a vigorous frenzy that accompanies every moment of digging. If you hear less barking but more whimpering, it means your companion might be in trouble, and digging quickly could save its life, especially because there's less air underground, and every passing moment could significantly weaken the dog, allowing the fox to gain the upper hand.

Depth is another adversary, the farther you hear the barking, the faster you need to dig, but you must always be careful not to cause a collapse of the soil. Fatigue in digging is felt almost immediately, your arms start to ache, and your hands can't grip as well as at the beginning of the excavation. It's not guaranteed that you'll only encounter soil while digging; there are also rocks and roots in your way, along with many other things that often slow down the pace.

The bond between the terrierman and his terrier is crucial at this critical moment. The camaraderie between the two is essential to work in harmony and achieve the common

Correct digging with the terrier recovery and reaching the fox.

goal: capturing the fox. The shared commitment, collective effort, and intense emotions culminate in the success of the hunt. When the terrier is finally released and the fox is captured, the sense of accomplishment and satisfaction is immense.

Bolting a fox

In fox hunting, the "bolting" moment represents a crucial and exhilarating phase of the entire experience. Once the fox has taken refuge in its den, the hunters must carefully plan how to flush it out to initiate the pursuit or capture.
The use of terriers is one of the most traditional and effective methods for bolting a fox. Thanks to their boldness and agility, terriers can either chase the fox away or keep it occupied, urging it to seek an escape route. Once the terrier has been sent into the den, the hunters listen attentively, anxious to hear the signals indicating that the fox has been forced out of the den and that the hunt can continue.
It is an ancient practice that requires a combination of skills and strategy from both hunters and their hunting dogs. After bolting, the fox is chased through various

Fox in den ready to jump out

types of terrain, such as woods, open fields, and hilly landscapes. The hunters move swiftly, following the cues of the hunting dogs that tirelessly work to keep track of the fox.

Fox hunting is an activity that demands proper preparation, respect for the environment, and consideration for the animals involved. It is a tradition deeply rooted in rural culture and continues to be practiced by many hunting enthusiasts around the world.

In the context of "bolting" during fox hunting, the use of a net is a traditional method to capture the fox as it emerges from its den. The net is a specialized tool strategically positioned over the den's exit to trap the fox at the moment it attempts to escape. The terrierman's skill lies in

Net positioned at the den exit

identifying the various entrances to the fox dens in the days leading up to the hunt and taking steps to block some exits in order to position the net precisely where the fox is expected to emerge. This means that the terrierman is an expert in the surrounding territory and well acquainted with the habits and characteristics of the wild.

The net used for capturing the fox is made of a durable and lightweight fabric, typically nylon or similar material. It is designed with a system of ropes and rings that allow it to be opened and closed quickly. The net is placed over the den's exit to form a barrier that prevents the fox from passing through it once it has been pushed out. When the fox escapes from the exit, the cords surrounding the exit quickly close over the fox, trapping it inside. Once the fox is caught in the net, the hunters can approach cautiously and proceed to capture it safely. This may involve the use of protective gloves and appropriate tools to prevent injuries to both the fox and the hunters themselves. The fox is then removed from the net and can be handled. In some situations, the fox is released again to be hunted in the future, while in others, it may be taken into custody for population control or other purposes.

Bolting a fox represents a true challenge for hunters and terriermen, as well as a demonstration of the training and working abilities of the terriers. These dogs, with their boldness, digging skills, and hunting instinct, are capable of facing one of the most intelligent prey in the animal kingdom.

The Terrierman

From the city to the countryside, the terrier has always been a useful companion for a thousand reasons. Even when it came to fox hunting on horseback, they were bred as an essential support. Their care and selection, based on qualities, terrain, and the type of hunting to be undertaken, were entrusted to the terrierman. He was a professional who worked in service of the Gentlemen's Clubs, the associations for fox hunting on horseback, also known as Hunts.

He was entrusted with two specific tasks: the first involved inspecting the hunting area and flushing out as many foxes as possible the day before the hunt, using terriers alternately, preventing their re-entry, and giving the hunting group the chance to spot them in the woods. The terrierman would close the entrances of the dens to prevent the foxes from seeking refuge during the hunt and, if necessary, would extract the fox from the den with the help of a dog, in cases where the terrain had not been surveyed in advance.

The second task was during the hunt itself. The possibility that the fox might find refuge in dens where the hounds could not enter was not so remote, and the terrierman's task was to flush them out for the continuation of the hunt, using the terrier's assistance.

Not being as fast as the horse or the hounds, the Russell Terrier was often transported in saddlebags.

Fox hunting represents a long tradition in England, and terriermen play a fundamental role in this practice. These figures are highly skilled and possess extensive knowledge of terrier and fox behavior, in addition to being

experts in training and handling dogs. Thanks to their experience, they can accurately assess the abilities of terriers and select the most suitable ones for the hunt.

Their ability to assess the terrain is of crucial importance, as it allows them to identify fox tracks and determine the location of their dens. This skill is essential for successfully guiding the group of hunters and dogs during the hunt.

In addition to terriers, they have a few but effective tools at their disposal that aid them in fox hunting. Among these, we can mention:

Excavation equipment: such as shovels, picks, and other necessary tools for digging around the fox den.

Protective clothing: like gloves and boots, to safeguard them during the hunt and excavation.

Iron stakes: these are long metal bars used to block the fox once it has been located or to gauge the depth of the den.

The expertise in handling dogs and the experience in hunting make the terrierman a respected figure within the hunting community. Some of them take pride in competing with each other in digging competitions, attempting to dig as deep as possible into the ground to find the quarry. This digging competition is considered a fun and stimulating experience.

However, it's important to note that the behavior of terriermen, especially in the context of fox hunting, is often considered cruel and, in many cases, illegal. During underground hunting, both the terriers and the prey, such as foxes or badgers, can sustain severe injuries. Dogs can get hurt in the narrow dens, struggling with roots and spikes on the tunnel walls, or even facing the prey itself. In a direct encounter, along with the terrier's skills, experience plays a fundamental role in ensuring the successful and unharmed outcome of the hunt.

Injuries suffered by terriers and prey can be serious and require proper veterinary care. Due to some hunters' reluctance to seek a veterinarian or lack of proper medical knowledge, attempts to treat wounds may be carried out without anesthesia or competence, causing further suffering to the involved animals.

It's not uncommon for contemporary terriermen to try to treat their dog's wounds with fabric glue or resort to any method to avoid going to the vet. Even industry magazines, like the Countryman's Weekly, have recently advertised "Skin Staplers" (a type of glue) to "repair small cuts and lacerations. Ideal for working dogs", all to avoid difficult questions from the vet. Other terriers remain trapped or lost underground for days, and in some cases, the dog may simply suffocate.

Some of the most famous terriermen in the history of fox hunting in England include Reverend John Russell, also known as "Jack", Bowman, and Heinemann. These men were experts in using terriers for fox and badger hunting and were respected and admired within the canine community and society. Their experience and skill in training and using terriers for fox and badger hunting have made them significant figures in the history of English hunting.

Many of them have become thought leaders and popular figures in the hunting world, with commendable knowledge and extensive experience in terrier use. They are often respected and admired by the hunting community and have been able to pass on their knowledge and skills to many new generations of terriermen. These individuals are important as they keep hunting traditions alive and promote their continuity through education and training.

The difference between 19th-century terriermen and those of today is significant. 19th-century terriermen were primarily engaged in fox hunting, which was then a common and accepted activity in England. These were usually men who lived in the countryside and had a deep understanding of fox habits and hunting techniques. They also had a strong relationship with their dogs, which were often bred for this specific purpose.

Contemporary terriermen, on the other hand, are often fox hunting enthusiasts who practice it as a hobby since fox hunting has been banned in many countries, including England and Wales. Nowadays, they focus on training and educating terriers, which are often used for badger hunting and other animals. Furthermore, modern terriermen are often members of clubs and organizations that support this passion and promote the health and well-being of terriers.

The saddlebag

Carrying the small terriers in the saddlebag during fox hunting was a very common practice in the past and offered numerous advantages to the hunters. Firstly, terriers were small-sized dogs, lightweight and agile, which could be easily transported in the saddlebag or specially designed pockets. This allowed hunters to always have their valuable hunting dogs at hand, ready for action when needed.

One of the main reasons for carrying terriers in the saddlebag was to protect them during the initial stages of the hunt. Before letting the terriers enter the fox dens, hunters initiated the hunt using tracking dogs to drive the fox towards an open area where it could be spotted by the mounted hunters. During this phase, the terriers were not directly involved and were kept in the saddlebag to prevent them from dispersing or getting accidentally injured during the movement of horses and tracking dogs. Furthermore, by keeping the terriers in the saddlebag, hunters could have better control over their dogs, ensuring they were ready to enter the dens when required. Another reason for carrying terriers in the saddlebag was to prevent them from engaging in unwanted actions during the hunt. Terriers were extremely bold, brave, and impulsive dogs, known for their strong determination to hunt and confront prey. Fox hunting required precise strategy and proper control of the dogs. Keeping the terriers in the saddlebag allowed hunters to have more direct control over their dogs, preventing them from chasing the fox prematurely.

During the hunt, terriers could be exposed to rugged terrain, natural obstacles, adverse weather conditions, and other dangers that could jeopardize their safety. The saddlebag provided a protective barrier that reduced the risk of injuries or accidents while navigating challenging terrains.

Carrying the terriers in the saddlebag was also a practice that reflected the affection and importance hunters attributed to their dogs. Terriers were considered an integral part of the fox hunting experience and were treated with great care and respect.

Innate Passion for Hunting

This breed is known for its courage, agility, and above all, its sharp hunting instinct. The hunting instinct of the Russell Terrier is an innate characteristic that manifests in many aspects of its behavior, making it an excellent hunting dog. It's important to remember that for dogs, surviving in nature involves hunting and preying for sustenance, as it's part of their primal instinct.

The hunting instinct of the Russell Terrier has deep roots in its history and original purpose. An agile, brave dog that could enter dens to flush out the fox or confront it in a direct encounter.

Rock den exit
(Parson Russell Terrier - Mambo's Gunner del Gatol)

The hunting instinct manifests in many typical behaviors of this breed, such as prey detection, chasing, barking, and occasionally digging.

Prey Detection: The terrier possesses a highly developed sense of smell and a great ability to detect prey, whether it's a fox, rodent, or any other animal. When a terrier enters a den, its sense of smell becomes its primary guide. The odors left by the prey, such as its body, secretions, and tracks, remain inside the den, creating a labyrinth of trails to follow. Thanks to its extraordinary olfactory sensitivity, the terrier can detect even the faintest odors, allowing it to precisely track the path of the prey within the den.

Differences in the type of underground terrain can influence the terrier's ability to detect and follow the prey. In tighter and more intricate dens, odors can be more concentrated and recognizable, making the dog's work easier. Conversely, in larger and more complex dens, odors can be more dispersed and confused, requiring the terrier to pay greater attention and dedication in identifying the tracks.

The time of day and seasons can also play a role in underground hunting. During the cooler hours of the morning or evening, the humidity in the air can help keep odors inside the den, facilitating the dog's sense of smell.

On hot or dry days, however, odors can dissipate more quickly, making the hunt more challenging.

In any case, the terrier must rely on its olfactory ability, guided by its hunting instinct, to detect and track the prey underground. The training and experience of the terrierman are crucial in developing the dog's abilities to best use its sense of smell during the underground hunt, ensuring the success of the hunting activity. Additionally, their vision is sensitive to movement and can spot their prey even at a distance, following it with determination.

Chasing: Chasing is one of the innate and most powerful characteristics of dogs, especially working dogs like terriers. When a terrier detects prey, a primal instinct is activated that drives it to engage in a relentless pursuit. From that moment, the dog enters a state of excitement and determination, ready to run with great speed and agility to catch its prey. The scene is captivating to observe: the terrier harnesses its muscular power and explosive energy, launching itself into the chase with unstoppable determination. Its focus is at its peak, all other thoughts fade away, and the sole objective is to reach and seize the prey. The chasing instinct is closely connected to the hunting instinct, which is embedded in the dog's DNA from ancient times. This behavior was crucial for the survival of their ancestors, and even today, terriers retain this ancestral instinct. When a terrier sets off in pursuit, the terrierman must allow this instinct to take over and respect its nature as a hunter. It's an impressive and engaging sight, but it's essential that the dog is appropriately guided, trained, and encouraged to engage in this behavior. The chasing instinct makes terriers exceptional hunting companions and loyal friends for those who love hunting. Their passion for hunting is one of the distinctive traits of this breed and makes them extraordinarily rewarding dogs to have by one's side during hunting expeditions.

Barking: it's one of the Russell Terrier's secret weapons when underground in search of prey. This vocal characteristic is crucial for communicating with the terrierman and signaling its position and the presence of the prey. The terrier's bark must be distinct and recognizable so that the terrierman can immediately understand that the dog has located the fox and has begun the pursuit.

To be effective, the Russell Terrier's bark must possess certain specific qualities. Firstly, it should be rhythmic, emitted at regular intervals. This allows the terrierman to easily recognize its sound and distinguish it from any environmental noises or the barks of other dogs present on the scene. An irregular or confused bark could confuse the terrierman and make it harder to locate the terrier and the prey.

Additionally, the bark should be loud and piercing. Given the nature of subterranean hunting, it's essential that the terrierman can clearly hear the bark even through the thick layer of earth that separates the terrier from the surface. Only a bark with a strong and distinct timbre can travel through the soil and effectively reach the terrierman.

The Russell Terrier's bark is a genuine form of communication between the dog and the terrierman. The terrierman must interpret the bark of their companion to understand the type of situation unfolding underground. Persistent and continuous barking might indicate that the terrier has located the prey and is chasing it, while less frenzied barking could suggest that the terrier hasn't yet found the fox. The importance of barking is also evident in competitions and working trials for terriers. During these activities, terriers are evaluated not only for their hunting abilities but also for the quality and effectiveness of their barking. A terrier with a powerful and well-structured bark demonstrates the right qualities to be a successful hunter and a reliable companion for the terrierman.

Digging: One of its distinctive traits is its skill in digging. This behavior is deeply rooted in its hunting instinct and reflects its nature as a working dog specialized in searching for and capturing animals that hide underground.

When the terrier detects the signal of its prey or senses the scent guiding it towards the target, enthusiasm takes over. With innate determination, the dog starts digging with passion and dedication, thrusting into the ground with great energy. This behavior is a direct result of its working dog genetics, developed over centuries to hunt animals like foxes, badgers, and other small creatures that seek refuge underground.

The Russell Terrier possesses considerable strength relative to its slim and compact body, allowing it to tackle compact and tough terrain with ease. This attribute makes it an excellent digger, capable of breaking through the ground swiftly and ferociously, driven to reach its prey.

Once the terrier begins to dig, its instinct and passion compel it to persist until it reaches its goal. It can dig rapidly and precisely, creating a passage through the ground that enables it to follow the prey into its den.

This digging prowess is a crucial feature for subterranean hunting, where the terrier must confront natural obstacles and often navigate through compact and tough ground. Without the ability to dig with determination, the terrier wouldn't be able to reach its prey, and its role as an underground hunter would be compromised. It's important to provide the terrier with appropriate opportunities to express this natural inclination.

From a young age, dogs play and engage in hunting actions with the pack, refining their visual, olfactory,

Puppy after playful digging
(Jack Russell Terrier - Chakys Jack Priamo)

stalking, chasing, and capturing skills, which are the distinct phases of their predatory instinct.

The Russell Terrier is known for their high energy levels and endurance. They express their instinct by hunting small prey on land and carrying out the action with the capture of the prey. With medium and large prey, they tend to signal or bark from a distance, attempting to attack only if they believe they have the upper hand.

Unlike other terriers, they avoid physical contact, as their primary role is to hold the prey at bay until the terrierman arrives. However, if forced into a confrontation, they won't back down and can fight with ferocity and tenacity, inflicting serious harm on their opponent.

In situations where the opponent is larger or the habitat is hostile, barking from a distance without direct contact can be a winning strategy for the terrier.

One peculiarity of this breed is their independence when facing a wild animal underground. The dog finds itself alone against its adversary, without the support of humans or the pack. This aspect may not be known or appreciated by many, but it's the result of selection that has made Russell Terriers fearless and insensitive to pain.

A content terrier is one that has had the opportunity to express its nature, both through play and through hunting activities. Allowing the dog to satisfy its instinct in a correct and lawful manner will contribute to making it more balanced. However, it's important to keep in mind that the dog's level of predatory instinct will influence the amount of work required to satisfy it appropriately.

Despite the Russell Terrier adapting well to indoor life, they are always eager to participate in offered activities, and their happiness will reflect yours. Remember, though, that your four-legged companion will need proper physical and mental activity to maintain a healthy emotional balance.

Work and Selection

In addition to being courageous, athletic, and bold, with a strong inclination to dig and pursue their prey, Russell Terriers had to possess morphological traits that suited their work underground. Work and selection played a fundamental role in the development of the breed. Dog owners selected the bravest and most athletic individuals for breeding, thus creating a breed of dogs highly efficient in hunting and capturing subterranean animals. Over time, these dogs also became popular as companion animals

Two puppies after having fun digging
(Jack Russell Terrier - Chakys Jack Spartaco e Chakys Jack Priamo)

due to their intelligence and affectionate and expressive nature.

The selection of terriers focused on creating strong, active, and brave dogs with exceptional digging and searching abilities. These traits were necessary to meet the needs of hunters and farmers, who required dogs capable of facing wild animals like badgers and foxes.

Throughout the centuries, terrier selection concentrated on creating breeds with specific physical and behavioral characteristics adapted to various tasks. For example, smaller terriers were developed for rodent hunting in confined spaces, while larger terriers were selected to tackle larger animals such as boars.

Today, terriers continue to be employed in various activities, including hunting, participating in obedience and agility competitions, dog shows, and as companion animals. However, terrier selection has also evolved to meet the needs of modern owners, who demand well-balanced and socialized dogs that are visually appealing as well.

Responsible selection is crucial to ensure that terrier breeds are healthy, balanced, and suitable for the tasks for which they were created. This entails selecting individuals with desirable physical and behavioral traits, as well as preventing the reproduction of individuals with health or behavioral problems. Choosing healthy subjects remains important to ensure that these breeds stay healthy, balanced, and suitable for their intended purposes. For instance, many terrier breeds are prone to common health issues such as patellar luxation and primary lens luxation. Therefore, selection should aim to prevent these health problems by choosing individuals with a family history free of these issues.

Behavior is another fundamental factor. Terriers, in general, are highly active and require a lot of physical and mental exercise to remain happy and balanced. They also need interaction with other dogs and people to maintain their emotional well-being. They need space to run and play outdoors, while others may be more suited to apartment living.

Of course, the terrier's work in a burrow or underground is a fundamental aspect of their selection. These breeds were originally chosen for their ability to dig and hunt in burrows or underground. This work required terriers to have a compact body, strong claws, solid musculature, and great physical endurance.

However, these traits are not sufficient to ensure that a terrier is suitable for underground work. Selection must also consider other factors, such as the terrier's ability to work in groups with other dogs, its skill in following its instincts, and its ability to adapt to extreme conditions underground.

To ensure that terriers are suitable for underground work, selection must be conducted carefully and precisely. Breeders must be aware of the traits that make a terrier suitable for subterranean work and should only select individuals that possess these traits. This will ensure that terriers can continue to perform this important work safely and efficiently, and that these breeds can be loved and appreciated for many generations to come.

The fox

It is now well known that the Russell Terrier was originally developed in 19th-century England as a fox hunting dog. They were known for their agility, speed, and courage in hunting, and were often used in pairs with other hunting dogs. They were also highly intelligent and easy to train, which made them popular among fox hunters.

On the other hand, the fox is an animal that has fascinated humans for centuries. Known for its cunning, beauty, and agility, the fox is a highly versatile animal capable of adapting to a wide range of habitats. It can thrive in both rural and urban environments, and this adaptability allows it to prosper in many parts of the world.

The fox is also a very agile and fast animal. Its slender and flexible body allows it to move easily through vegetation, climb obstacles, and maneuver with agility in dens. These physical characteristics make it a highly efficient animal in hunting and escaping predators. Foxes typically live alone or in pairs, and they are most active during the night. During the day, they rest and hide in dens or other safe shelters.

Known for its cunning and intelligence, the fox is able to learn quickly and adapt to its surroundings. This ability to learn makes it very efficient in hunting, surviving in hostile environments, and dealing with difficult situations, such as being chased by a Russell Terrier.

In the English countryside, there was only one species of fox, which did not differ from those in the lands near the sea except for its thinner legs, but it could not be defined as a separate species: the red fox.

The female fox (known as a vixen) generally mates in December or January. During this period, she seeks a suitable den, perhaps one previously adapted and widened by a rabbit for easier entry and exit, with enough supplies to feed herself and her potential offspring in even the worst situations.

After two months, four or five cubs are born, and for the first two weeks, the mother stays with them in the den to care for them. There are various reasons why the mother does not leave the den. The main one is that the cubs are born with their eyes closed and cannot regulate their body heat. Considering that these months are among the coldest, the sudden departure of the mother would almost certainly result in the death of one or more cubs. So, for the first fifteen days, the mother cares for the cubs and then moves them to the most inaccessible corner of the den and goes out to find fresh food. She does not move far from the den; in fact, she guards the entrance, making sure no one approaches. If something were to alarm her, she would go to great lengths to find another den in a shaded and hidden place and then move her cubs one by one.

At four weeks, the pups start to crawl and slowly come out of the den, and the mother begins to play with them to teach them the basics for a good future. Once they have learned the basics, the mother gradually brings mice, small birds, and other small animals and teaches them how to hunt and kill them. At six to seven weeks of age, about a month and a half, thanks to the mother's dedication, they will start hunting poultry in nearby farms, all in broad daylight when the hens and chickens are free to roam the fields. It's unlikely for the fox to find the opportunity to enter a poultry house at night, as access points like windows and doors will be well closed.

At two months, the cubs venture into the woods with the mother to hunt for moles or small animals. At five to six months, they are capable of defending themselves, and the mother separates from the group for their well-being.

The amount of damage a fox can do is often exaggerated compared to its daily needs, not for fun, but to maintain its health.

The foul odor emitted by a fox serves as a strong warning signal to all creatures of the forest.

A fox rarely hunts near its den; in fact, its instinct leads it to hunt in a distant location, as farmers or enemies might search for evidence of the crime in nearby areas.

The fox's den is a safe and comfortable refuge it uses for resting, feeding, and raising its cubs. To keep the den clean and comfortable, the fox invests a lot of time and attention in its care and maintenance. The den is regularly cleaned, with old materials being replaced by new ones, ensuring it's well-ventilated and maintains a consistent internal temperature.

The fox is also very cautious about the safety of its den and ensures it's well hidden and protected from predators.

The fox's den is usually located underground, and it digs it with its strong paws and sharp claws. It's capable of digging very deep and complex dens with multiple chambers and tunnels, making it safe from predators.

Being a very active animal that loves to explore its territory, the den must be strategically located to allow easy access to food and water sources.

The fox defends itself in its den in various ways, some of which include:

Narrow entrance: The den's entrance is usually narrow and protected, making it difficult for predators to access the interior.

Multiple tunnels: Foxes often dig more than one den, ensuring they always have an escape route in case of danger.

Digging techniques: The fox knows precisely how to dig its den to make it safe and protected. For instance, it may dig tunnels that end in an underground chamber, making it challenging for predators to reach it.

Speed and Agility: The fox is very fast and agile, allowing it to quickly flee from its den in case of danger.

Frequent Inspection: The fox is known to regularly explore its territory, enabling it to detect dangers in real-time and adequately prepare.

During fox hunting, terriers are typically sent into the fox's den to force it to come out.

Having a good understanding of fox habits helps the terrierman prepare the territory before the hunt begins.

Terriers that worked in the den during fox hunting could face various dangers that could lead to their death.

Here are some of the main causes of death for terriers in the den:

Claw or Fang Injuries: The fox is a very defensive animal that can inflict serious injuries on terriers with its sharp claws and fangs. The fox's bite is continuous and can vary in intensity and force depending on the situation. In general, they have a relatively small mouth with sharp and cutting teeth suitable for tearing the flesh of the animals they hunt.

If a fox feels threatened or provoked, it might bite in self-defense. The fox's bite can be painful and cause injuries, but it's rarely fatal. It's important to remember that foxes can carry diseases like rabies, so it's crucial to avoid getting too close or attempting to interact with them.

In general, it's better to maintain a safe distance and admire foxes from afar to avoid any risk of biting or disease transmission.

Suffocation: Terriers could get trapped in the den and suffocate due to a lack of air. This is where the chest size and shape, along with specific terrier training, become important.

Den Collapse: During digging, the den could collapse on terriers, causing injuries or death due to suffocation.

Diseases transmitted by wild animals: Terriers could contract diseases from foxes or other wild animals during the hunt. Exposed wounds could lead to the infiltration of germs and bacteria that contribute to the onset of infections and other diseases that could result in the terrier's death.

Diseases and infections transmitted by other terriers: Foxes are wild animals and, as such, are exposed to a range of diseases and infections. Some common diseases include rabies, tuberculosis, leishmaniasis, heartworm disease, leptospirosis, and dysentery. Additionally, foxes can be infected with parasites like fleas, ticks, and worms. It's important to note that most of these diseases can also be transmitted to humans, so avoiding close contact with infected foxes or those showing signs of illness is crucial. As a result of the previous point, being in a pack, terriers could also contract diseases or infections from other terriers during the hunt.

Physical Exhaustion: The demanding work and physical effort required for digging and confronting the fox could lead to exhaustion and, in some cases, the death of the terrier. There are stories of terriers staying underground with the fox for a couple of days. The terrier doesn't feel fatigue much and pain only slightly, making it more susceptible to exhaustion.

The fox is a demanding animal from the perspective of terrier work, and there is a high risk to the health and safety of those subjects working in the den during fox hunting. It's important for terriers to receive proper training that allows them to mitigate the risk of these dangers. Reverend John Russell, aside from his clerical work, loved fox hunting. He started hunting them in his youth and continued until his passing. He was also an expert terrier trainer and was renowned for his ability to select the right dogs for the job.

Foxes are still considered a pest and can cause significant damage to crops and livestock. Fox hunting helps control the fox population and also provides a valuable source of exercise for dogs.

The Badger

The tradition of badger hunting with terriers is deeply rooted in English culture and has given rise to many terrier breeds specialized in this activity, such as the Jack Russell Terrier, the Parson Russell Terrier, the Border Terrier, and the Norfolk Terrier.

The hunting activity involves tracking and capturing the badger, a nocturnal animal that lives in burrows dug into the ground. This type of hunting has been practiced for centuries in many parts of the world, but it originated in the United Kingdom, where Russell Terriers, due to their courage and strong predatory instinct, proved ideal for chasing and capturing an animal like the badger.

Also known as Meles meles, the badger is a wild animal belonging to the Mustelidae family. Shy and reluctant to socialize, the badger is a nocturnal creature. Its fur is thick and soft, with a gray color on the back, lighter on the sides, a white head with a characteristic black stripe on the sides. It possesses great strength and agility, enabling it to move quickly even in tight and difficult spaces. With short and sturdy legs equipped with sharp claws, it can easily dig into the ground and construct complex underground burrows, where it spends much of the day sheltered from the sun and potential predators.

Unlike the fox, the badger's burrow is generally less complex than that of the fox, as the badger is a less active animal. The badger's burrow consists of a series of underground galleries that extend beneath the ground, with separate entrances for entering and exiting, helping to maintain a consistent internal temperature. In contrast,

the fox's burrow is generally larger and more intricate, featuring multiple chambers extending underground.

To distinguish between a badger's burrow and a fox's burrow from the outside, there are several signs to consider. The badger's burrow is generally larger and has a wider entrance compared to that of the fox. Additionally,

Badger in rocky burrow

the main pathway of the badger's burrow is longer and is more likely to be located near a watercourse or in a swampy area, while the fox prefers a higher and drier location.

The badger possesses a strong jaw and sharp teeth, enabling it to grip and drag heavy prey. It has a wide variety of dietary habits, ranging from fruits, berries, and roots to meat and many other sources of food. It's a curious and lively animal that often explores its territory and surroundings in search of food. However, if it feels threatened, it becomes immediately aggressive and defends its burrow fiercely. The badger is determined and stubborn, meaning that once it initiates a hunt, it won't easily give up.

The badger is also known for marking its territory with its odoriferous secretions, released through glands present on its body. This allows it to communicate with other individuals of the same species and signal its presence to others. It's a solitary animal that tends to live alone, except during the mating season. During this period, males and females come together for brief periods to mate and then separate once again.

The badger hunt in 19th century England was widespread and considered a true sport. The badger was a sought-after prey for its fur and meat, as well as for its status as a wild and unpredictable animal. During the badger hunt, hunters used specially trained dogs that followed the scent of the animal to its burrow and entered to flush it out. Once out, the badger was chased by the dogs and hunters.

During the hunt, the dog is exposed to numerous risks and dangers that can cause injuries. For example, the burrows where the badger takes refuge can be very narrow and winding, with the presence of roots, rocks, and other natural obstacles that can cause wounds. Additionally, the badger can exhibit aggressive behaviors and defend itself. The badger's claws are sharp and robust, and can pose a serious danger. The length can vary, but on average it's about 2-3 centimeters, which is crucial for digging burrows and defending against attackers, so they are naturally sharp and sturdy.

When a hunting dog pursues the badger into its burrows, the badger can use its claws to defend itself and attack the dog, causing scratches and deep wounds that can be very painful. In particular, the badger's claws can pose a danger to exposed parts of the dog, such as its eyes, ears, and neck.

The badger was also called "Gray", from the old name of Devonshire, as many of those animals had long occupied that place.

Reverend John Russell was passionate about fox hunting, but after his death, Arthur Blake Heinemann took on a significant role in promoting badger hunting. In 1894, he founded the Devon and Somerset Badger Club, an association dedicated specifically to badger hunting and the selection of terriers suitable for this purpose.

Born in 1867 in Gillingham, Dorset, England, Heinemann had a deep interest in hunting and dog breeding from a young age. He dedicated himself to developing a breed of terrier particularly suitable for badger hunting. He was actively involved in creating the breed standard for the Jack Russell Terrier, which defined the ideal characteristics in terms of size, coat, structure, and temperament for badger hunting.

The Devon and Somerset Badger Club, founded by Heinemann, played a fundamental role in spreading interest in the Russell Terrier and solidifying its reputation as a hunting dog specialized in badger hunting.

Despite his death in 1928, Arthur Blake Heinemann's legacy in creating the breed standard for the Jack Russell Terrier and his commitment to badger hunting continue to influence the history of this breed and the community of hunting dog enthusiasts.

Training Initiation

Terriers are known for their extraordinary ability to infiltrate underground to reach their prey and for the variety of methods they use to capture it, such as scaring it, nipping it, or biting it. Additionally, they are skilled at dragging the prey out of the burrow or guiding it into a trap to catch it.

Training Terriers is of fundamental importance to fully utilize their hunting abilities. Starting training from a young age is essential, as delaying it could prevent them from developing the ability to enter underground and therefore carry out their role as hunters. During training, it's important to be patient, consistent, and reward the dog for desired behaviors.

Gameness, a term associated with various hunting dog breeds, including some terriers like the Russell Terrier, is an important concept to consider. It represents the dog's determination, courage, and perseverance in facing a challenge or opponent, even in extremely difficult situations.

Once training is completed, the dog should be able to face the wild on its own. Its ability to handle future situations and its ability to manage will depend precisely on its gameness.

It shouldn't be confused with aggressive or dangerous behaviors; gameness is rather a quality that allows the dog to persevere and face challenges with courage, but it must always be directed towards legitimate activities like hunting and adequately controlled by the terrierman. Dogs with gameness are known for their resilience and determination, pushing themselves to the limit to achieve their goal. This characteristic was originally selected in some breeds for combat activities, where endurance and the will to continue despite adversity were considered relevant.

It's important to emphasize that the concept of gameness is controversial and debated within the dog community. The idea of combat dogs and encouraging aggressive behaviors is not supported or promoted by most trainers and animal lovers.

Today, gameness is generally associated with a mental attitude and predisposition of the dog to fully engage in an activity, such as hunting work. This doesn't mean that the dog should be involved in fights or dangerous situations, but rather that it has a strong will and great commitment to completing the assigned task.

Gameness can be expressed through the dog's focus, energy, and dedication in pursuing a goal. For example, a committed Jack Russell Terrier in hunting might show great determination in following a trail or chasing prey, demonstrating remarkable physical and mental resilience. A dog with gameness can be highly motivated and focused, but should always be appropriately trained and responsibly managed to ensure its safety and that of others.

It's crucial to respect and understand the innate characteristics of a breed, including the inclination for gameness, but also to ensure that the dog's training and socialization are balanced and directed towards legal and safe activities, such as search work or other disciplines suitable for the breed.

There are several ways to achieve this goal: starting with specific training focused on the hunting skills for which the dog has been selected. This can include basic commands,

Young subject in training with a fox tail.
(Jack Russell Terrier - Chakys Jack Van Helsing)

track searching, prey retrieval, and other skills necessary for hunting.

Socialization is crucial: expose the dog to various situations, people, dogs, and animals from a young age. This helps develop appropriate social skills and accustom the dog to different stimuli.

Gradually introduce the dog to simulated hunting situations. Use objects that resemble the scent and appearance of real prey to increase the Russell Terrier's interest in hunting and improve its tracking abilities. You can use an object that simulates prey and carries its scent, such as a fox tail, encouraging the dog to chase it, bark, and attempt to seize it. Familiarizing the dog with the scents of the game it will be seeking is essential. Wild animal skins can be used to create positive associations with hunting scents. The dog can be encouraged to play and search for these skins, thereby associating the scent

with reward. This develops the dog's attention, motivation, search skills, and in the case of play, speed and agility.

Gradual progression in training: increase the difficulty as the dog acquires skills. Transition to more complex prey or simulated hunting situations as the dog develops mental resilience and required determination.

There are several techniques to train Terriers subsequently and ensure they are capable hunters. For instance, one of the most common techniques involves introducing an older Terrier into the underground burrow. This way, young Terriers can learn from the experienced dog's example on how to bark and hunt. It's important to reward Terriers for their hard work by offering them rewards such as food, liver, fat, ears, or the skin of the conquered prey.

This helps strengthen their hunting instinct and maintain their motivation.

Then, proceed with the introduction to the artificial burrow. Create an environment resembling an underground den, where the dog learns to chase and confront the prey. This can be done using pipes or other structures simulating underground conditions. The dog is encouraged to enter the den and follow the scent of the prey.

Positive reinforcements are essential: use praise and positive reinforcements to reward the dog when it shows gameness and desired behaviors during training or hunting. This reinforces the positive association between desired behavior and reward.

It's always important to emphasize that the development of gameness must not encourage aggressive or dangerous behavior. Safety for the dog and others is always a priority during training and hunting.

While known for their ability to hunt underground, such as capturing foxes and badgers in dens, Russell Terriers are equally skilled in surface hunting.

In surface hunting, Terriers use their keen sense of smell and agility to locate and chase prey on the ground. They can be trained to hunt a variety of game, such as rabbits, hares, and other small creatures that move on the ground's surface.

During surface hunting, Terriers display a strong chasing instinct and a great desire to catch the prey. They are renowned for their speed, agility, and determination in pursuing the prey through obstacles like bushes, rocks, and rough terrain.

Terrier trainers invest time and energy into developing the dogs' surface hunting skills. This may involve training to follow the wild animal's track, obedience training, recall training, as well as practical experience in field hunting. During surface hunting, Terriers work closely with their handler, who can provide guidance and instructions during the pursuit of the prey. Surface hunting offers a stimulating challenge for the Terrier, allowing them to showcase their natural abilities and make the most of their hunting instincts.

Russell Terriers are highly versatile dogs that excel in both surface and underground hunting. Their agility, speed, and determination make them perfect for tackling a wide range of prey on the ground's surface, significantly contributing to the success of hunting sessions. While surface hunting differs from underground work, both activities complement each other in various aspects, providing the dog with greater motivation, a more developed predatory instinct, and improved searching abilities.

Instinct Tests for Earthdog Breeds

There are tests designed to assess the natural abilities of our terrier, whether it's a Jack Russell or a Parson Russell terrier, by analyzing its response to wild animals.

In Australia, the country of origin of the Jack Russell Terrier, the "earthdog instinct test" is used. The "Earthdog" instinct test is an assessment that evaluates the natural underground working instincts of terriers. This test was developed to assess a terrier's abilities in locating, tracking, and capturing prey underground, such as foxes and badgers.

During the test, the dog is taken to an artificial den or a system of underground tunnels where a prey (usually a rat) or its scent has been placed. The goal is to observe how the dog reacts and utilizes its hunting instincts to locate and confront the prey within the underground environment.

This test can provide terrier owners with an opportunity to discover if their dog possesses a strong hunting instinct and a predisposition for underground work. It's important to emphasize that this test evaluates the dog's natural instinct only and is not comprehensive training to become a professional hunting dog.

In England, the country of origin of the Parson Russell Terrier, there's a similar test called the "Working Terrier Assessment" (WTA), specifically designed for working terriers. The WTA is a test intended to evaluate terriers' hunting skills, including underground hunting. The test is conducted by various canine organizations in the United Kingdom, such as the Working Terrier Club, and aims to identify and assess the qualities of a terrier in practical hunting contexts.

During the test, terriers are evaluated on various aspects, including their ability to locate and confront prey in artificial dens, determination in tracking the prey's trail, ability to overcome obstacles, and cooperation with other hunting dogs. The WTA puts terriers' natural abilities and training to the test in a real hunting scenario.

In Italy, a similar test is called the "Test of Natural Attitude" (TAN). The test is designed to assess the natural hunting abilities of terriers, where dogs are exposed to different simulated situations with the presence of prey such as guinea pigs, rabbits, foxes, and wild boars, in order to evaluate their abilities to locate, track, and confront prey.

Participating in instinct and hunting attitude tests, even if simulated, provides terrier owners with a unique opportunity to evaluate their dogs' hunting capabilities and connect with fellow terrier enthusiasts. These social events are a beginning to promote the conservation of terrier breeds and keep alive the hunting traditions rooted in their history.

The preparation of the testing field is of paramount importance. The field is selected and set up to recreate a natural and realistic environment that can challenge the dogs' abilities. During the tests, there's an increasing level of visual stimulation and challenge, providing the opportunity to assess the dogs' courage in various situations, responding to the visual and olfactory stimuli generated by the wild animals. The dog's approach, tone of voice, and temperament are carefully evaluated. For example, a dog with a consistent bark and tone is

Wild boar test
(Jack Russell Terrier - Chakys Jack Perfect Harmony)

preferred over a dog with a shrill and irregular tone. All these characteristics are part of the overall assessment.

These tests are particularly suitable for very young dogs or those that have never had experiences with wild animals, or those that have not been previously trained for artificial den hunting. They provide an excellent starting point to develop the innate qualities of Terriers, but it's important to remember that they are just the beginning of the journey. These tests give us the necessary incentive to continue progressing gradually. We must climb the steps one after the other without stopping because a dog's behavior when facing wildlife on the ground, in a controlled and familiar environment, is different from what it might exhibit in a confined space, face to face with a fox. To succeed, we must grow as owners and adopt an approach aimed at nurturing the specific character of Terriers. Only in this way can we preserve the incredible spirit that characterizes our fascinating companion, the Terrier.

Artificial or playful den work tests

Throughout history, utility dogs have played a significant role in hunting and territory protection. Through close interaction with humans, they have specialized in various tasks. In the case of Jack and Parson Russell Terriers, their natural qualities emerge through work tests, which aim to identify suitable individuals, highlighting their qualities and canine value. In this chapter, we specifically focus on artificial or underground den work tests, examining the test environment and the competition field in detail.

In Australia, there are various tests based on the terrier's abilities. Among these, the Senior and Master tests are considered particularly important to assess the attitudes of Russell Terriers.

The Senior Test is designed to simulate a real hunting situation, providing the owner with a more realistic experience. The den used in this test represents a complex environment with multiple entrances, similar to natural dens found in the wild. This test aims to evaluate the dog's ability to track the prey, determine the correct direction taken by it, and leave the den when called by the hunter. Passing the Senior Test requires the dog to demonstrate skill and competence in dealing with a complex den.

In real hunting, dens are not simple tunnels but often have elaborate configurations with multiple entrances. Dogs must show their ability to track the prey until they signal its presence to the handler or owner. Additionally, they must be able to determine the correct direction taken by the prey if it has escaped. When called, the dogs must exit the den.

Entrance of an artificial den

The test is divided into three main parts: approaching the prey, working on the prey, and exiting the den on command.

Regarding the den's design, it is constructed using standard linings that form a main tunnel with 90-degree turns, a false bed (also called an oven). The false exit is positioned in a way that is not visible to the dog or handler when they are at the release point. The false oven, on the other hand, is a side tunnel with no exit that ends with a bed and a door placed at the top.

To simulate the nesting area present in most natural dens, a pile of strongly scented bedding material is placed under the entrance of the den.

During the test, the handler brings the dog to the entrance of the test area and, upon the Judge's instruction, releases the dog. "Throwing" (pushing) the dog in the direction of the den entrance is prohibited. The handler can provide unlimited verbal encouragement but cannot move beyond the den entrance or touch the dog or equipment.

Prove di ingresso del terrier in tana artificiale
(Jack Russell Terrier - Alcor)

The timing for the approach to the quarry begins when the dog is released and has 90 seconds to reach the quarry. Once the quarry is reached, the dog must stay with it for the completion of the working part of the test. If the dog leaves the quarry area during the test, it will not pass. The dog has 15 seconds to start working once the quarry is reached, otherwise, it will not qualify.

Working on the quarry is defined as barking, growling, digging, or any other form of activity indicating the dog's interest in the quarry. The dog must work continuously on the quarry for at least 60 seconds. During this phase, the Judge may try to engage the dog without penalizing it, using manipulation of the quarry, noises, or vocal encouragements. The important thing is that the dog maintains attention on the quarry and continues to work for at least 60 seconds. Any change in the form of work or activity is not considered a pause. Jumps and removal of earth are considered part of the work, while intense staring or sniffing of the quarry is not considered work.

Once the working part of the test is completed, the Judge seals the area and removes the quarry to prevent distractions. Subsequently, the handler is instructed to call the dog back. The handler can approach the den entrance and use a whistle to recall the dog, but using food, noises, or toys to lure the dog out of the den is not allowed. The handler can retrieve the dog once it exits the den within 90 seconds of the recall. If the dog takes more than 90 seconds to exit the den, it will not pass the test.

After successfully completing all three parts of the Senior Test, dogs that have qualified are announced by the Judge. The organizing club of the test may award prizes or trophies to the qualified dogs.

This type of test aims to evaluate the competency and skills of the hunting dog in facing a complex den situation, similar to those encountered during a real hunt. It offers an opportunity for handlers to test and enhance their dogs' abilities in locating and tracking quarry, working on the quarry, and responding to owner's commands.

Hunting activities must be conducted ethically and in accordance with laws and conservation regulations.

Handlers are required to follow all regulations and adopt sustainable practices to ensure the conservation of species and natural habitats.

The transition to the Master Test best simulates a natural hunting situation. During an actual hunt, it is expected that the dog identifies the den and enters without encouragement. It must remain in the den and work on the quarry so that the hunter can locate both the dog and the quarry.

The artificial den of the Senior test is used, with some modifications. The entrance of the den must not be easily visible and must be blocked by an object that the dog can move to enter, such as a burlap flap, loose grass, or other elements that can conceal the entrance. An odor line of about 20 feet (6 meters) will lead to the entrance. In the middle of the odor line, a false den entrance will be placed, visible to the dogs, and at least 5 feet (1.5 meters) away from the odor line.

In the tunnel, at least two of the following obstacles must be present, positioned 5 feet (1.5 meters) from the entrance or the quarry:

(a) A tunnel narrowing consisting of boards or slats about 1.5 inches (3.8 cm) wide and 18 inches (45.6 cm) long, placed opposite each other to narrow the tunnel opening to about 6 inches (15.2 cm). The ends of the boards or slats must be chamfered or rounded.

(b) The obstacle consists of a tube with a diameter of 6 inches (15.2 cm) placed transversely in the tunnel and loosely fixed on a 1-inch (2.54 cm) pin, so that it can move (it should move about 2.5 inches or 6.3 cm in both directions). The part of the lining above the obstacle (9 inches or 22.8 cm on each side of the tube's centerline, totaling 18 inches or 45.6 cm) is raised at least 6 inches

(15.2 cm) above the main lining and is naturally covered or camouflaged.

(c) The curtain obstacle consists of a 9-inch (22.8 cm) wide board by 18 inches (45.6 cm) long, through which at least 30 9-inch (22.8 cm) long flags are threaded. The flags are made of thin flexible tubes no wider than 5 mm. This board replaces the roof of a section of the tunnel, with the flags hanging vertically.

(d) The sand pile obstacle consists of damp sand formed into a solid shape, creating a pile about 9 inches (22.8 cm) wide and 6 inches (15.2 cm) high, leaving a space of about 3 inches (7.6 cm) between the top of the pile and the tunnel's roof.

In short, the Master Earthdog Test has been designed to replicate a natural hunting situation. The dog must locate the den without encouragement, remain inside, and work on the quarry, allowing the handler to locate both the dog and the quarry itself. The tunnel used is similar to that of the Senior test but with modifications to the den entrance and the presence of at least two obstacles like the narrowing, tube obstacle, and sand pile obstacle. These obstacles make the test more challenging and require the dog to overcome various challenges during the tunnel course.

In Italy, the test of working ability and hunting attitude is carried out in an isolated location, preferably in an underbrush. The access key for all working tests is represented by gunshot. It's important to emphasize that a dog that does not pass the gunshot test will not be allowed to participate in any other working test.

In the working tests, two shots are initially fired from a distance using a blank-loaded pistol or rifle. The dogs, which can be kept on a leash or left free by the handler's side, must demonstrate that they are not afraid or fearful in the presence of gunfire.

Subsequently, the den test is conducted. The den should reflect, as much as possible, the burrows that foxes dig or use in nature and simulates the terrier's work inside the den itself. To ensure comfort and better control of training and circumstances, the test field is constructed by digging tracks with a depth of 20 centimeters and a width of 18 centimeters. These tracks are covered with hinged lids for easy maintenance.

The intersections between the tracks involve excavating a circular area called the "den", which is also buried and equipped with easily accessible hinged covers. Slots will be made in the entrance to insert grids that prevent the dog from coming into direct contact with the quarry.

During the journey inside these artificial burrows, the dogs will encounter various challenges, such as inclines that force them to descend and ascend compared to the normal plane of the burrows, and a "ditch" or hole that the dog must cross or jump over. In addition to the entrance, the den will consist of multiple exits and passable galleries, and the judge will choose which path the dog should follow during the test.

The first working test involves passing the quarry through an empty den to evaluate the terrier's abilities in locating the wild animal.

The fox is introduced through the den entrance and will be led out through one of the two exit dens, at the judge's discretion. Once it reaches the exit den, the fox is placed in its "carrier" called the Box, positioned about a meter from the exit.

The dog, without hesitation and with determination, must enter the den and follow the same path taken by the fox.

Barking at the "box"
(Jack Russell Terrier - Chakys Jack Van Helsing)

Subsequently, it must exit without hesitation or fear from the point where the box is located. This test evaluates the dog's ability to enter the den decisively and without hesitation. Furthermore, the dog must navigate the entire path confidently and quietly, demonstrating courage and eagerness. Only a few barks of excitement along the route are allowed.

In summary, the first working test involves passing the fox through an empty den. This test aims to assess the dog's ability to enter the den with determination and navigate the route with confidence, displaying a quiet and resolute attitude.

The second test comprises a series of assessments related to the dog's work: Work at the First Den, Work at the Second Den, Maintaining the Trail, Work at the Terminal Den, Temperament and Physical Endurance, Voice Tone and Rhythm.

In the second test, the fox is introduced through the entrance and stopped at the first den. Separation grids are then positioned to isolate and secure the fox, ensuring no contact. The handler allows the dog to enter through the entrance, and it must enter without fear and with determination. The dog will follow the path to the first den, where it will encounter the grid, smell the wild animal, and perceive movements, alerting to the presence of the fox with continuous and rhythmic barks.

The dog's bark should be regular and continuous, with short pauses allowed. After the first bark, the dog must maintain the barking for about two minutes without hesitation. If the dog exits without completing the test, it will be penalized. After the two minutes, the fox is moved to the second den and made to traverse the tunnel, securing it in the same way as the first den. Once the fox is enclosed in the second den, the grid separating the dog from the fox in the first den is lifted, and the dog must follow the scent trail with enthusiasm and a desire to locate the wild animal. The path must be faced without hesitation or fear. Once reaching the grille of the second oven, the dog must bark to indicate the presence of the fox, using the same barking pattern as in the first oven. After two minutes, the judge will release the fox and guide

Earth mound (wall).

it along the path to one of the two final ovens, which is decided by the judge prior to the start of the trial.

Once the fox is enclosed in the final oven, the dog is released from the grille and must follow the track to the fork, following the scent left by the fox. If the dog were to make a wrong turn at the fork but immediately corrects it, it will still be penalized for not using its sense of smell to follow the fox's scent. However, if it goes off course by leaving the path, the dog will be disqualified. Upon reaching the grille, the dog must perform the same task as in the other two ovens. When the two-minute time period is over, the fox is removed, and the trial concludes as the dog exits the tunnel.

When evaluating temperament and physical endurance, the dog's character and willingness to work are taken into account. Lack of drive, irregular and inconsistent barking, inadequate physical endurance, and excessive hesitation throughout the course will result in penalties.

Regarding the tone and rhythm of the voice, the dog should emit audible and consistent barks from above ground that are continuous. It's important to note that the barking should indicate the presence of the fox underground and therefore needs to be audible. Regular and appropriate barking that suits the work being done will be evaluated positively.

In summary, the second trial comprises several phases. After introducing the fox at the entrance and stopping it at the first oven, the dog navigates the path following the scent and alerts the presence of the fox with its barking. Subsequently, the fox is moved to the second oven, and the dog must follow the scent to bark again and indicate its presence. Finally, the dog arrives at the fork, where it must correctly follow the scent left by the fox. Throughout these stages, the dog's temperament, physical endurance, tone, and rhythm of its voice are evaluated.

After successfully completing the tunnel work trial, the digging trial follows. This trial involves the fox passing along a predetermined and mandatory path until it reaches one of the ovens, typically the third one. Once it reaches the oven, the fox is secured, and in the tunnel leading to the oven, a "wall" of sand or soil is created, spanning around 50 cm. An opening of about 5 cm is left between the lid and the top of the wall.

The dog must enter the tunnel from the entrance, follow the path, approach the wall, and then dig. After overcoming the wall, it must reach the fox and bark. The barking signals the end of the trial. A dog that completes the trial within the set time limit, usually 5 minutes from entering the tunnel, is considered the winner.

As mentioned earlier, these trials aim to assess and test the terriers' aptitude for subterranean hunting and, consequently, for dealing with wild animals, in this case, the fox. The trials are conducted multiple times to allow for a more detailed evaluation of the dog's abilities.

It's important to emphasize that no artificial tunnel trial can fully replicate the complexity and danger of the work that a terrier faces in a natural den.

Natural dens present unique and unpredictable challenges. The subterranean environment is intricate and often labyrinthine, with winding passages and narrow spaces that require agility and dexterity from the terrier. Conditions can vary greatly, with obstacles like roots, rocks, and unstable terrain testing the dog's physical endurance and determination.

Moreover, the terrier encounters real wild animals inside the den. This adds an element of danger and unpredictability, as the fox or wild animal can react in unforeseen ways, such as fighting, fleeing, or hiding, testing the terrier's skill and ability to capture it.

Artificial tunnel trials provide a way to evaluate the terriers' capabilities and training, but it's crucial to understand that they cannot fully replicate the complexity and challenge found in the natural environment. They offer an opportunity to assess attitude, courage, and workability, but they don't replace the experience and practice in real dens.

Therefore, while artificial tunnel trials are valuable for evaluating terrier abilities, it's important to recognize that the true test of skill and courage occurs in direct encounters with natural dens.

It should be noted that artificial den work trials can vary from one country to another. For further details, we recommend referring to the local canine society.

Work in the natural den

In the terrier's work within the natural den, the dog demonstrates a deep connection with its instincts and predator nature. It's a captivating experience to witness how the terrier adapts and moves gracefully through the subterranean environment, leveraging its skills to the fullest.

The natural den presents a series of unique challenges that the terrier must face. The tunnels can be intricate and winding, requiring the dog to navigate through narrow passages, steep curves, and complex intersections. The terrier's ability to maneuver with agility and grace in these

Exit from the natural den
(Parson Russell Terrier - Dido del Gatol)

confined spaces is impressive, showcasing its adaptability and bodily control.

The terrier heavily relies on its senses to tackle work within the natural den. Its highly developed sense of smell allows it to detect the tracks of the wild animal, accurately following them even in the presence of other scents within the subterranean environment. This tracking ability is crucial for locating and getting closer to the wild animal. The terrier's hearing is equally important, as it can pick up on sounds and movements of the animal hiding in the depths of the den.

Once the terrier has reached the animal within the den, the challenge of the physical confrontation begins. During the encounter with the wild animal, the terrier

Den with roots
(Parson Russell Terrier - Victor of Gatol)

demonstrates extraordinary determination and courage. Training and innate instinct enable it to face the animal with a combination of strength, cunning, and swiftness. Despite its smaller size compared to the wild animal, the terrier launches itself with boldness and tenacity, attempting to take control of the situation.

The struggle within the den can be a test of endurance and ferocity. The terrier employs its powerful musculature and tenacity to confront the animal, pushing it further inside and leaving little room for retreat. It's remarkable to see how the terrier manages to maintain its barking and perseverance despite the confined spaces and limited air both animals have to contend with.

Concentration and composure are essential to maintain control and make quick and effective decisions. The terrier must be able to instinctively assess the situation and react accordingly, always with the goal of cornering the wild animal in a corner of the den, awaiting the arrival of the terrierman.

In working with the wild, it doesn't matter whether you are a male or female terrier. The terrier's work in the natural den is a testament to its innate skill and dedication in fulfilling its role as a hunter, but it also represents the selection of many breeders who have appreciated and selected the hunting qualities of the terrier. It's an extraordinary experience to see how the dog immerses itself completely in the underground environment, making the most of its physical and mental abilities to achieve its goal. It showcases the incredible potential of this breed to hunt and confront wild animals. It highlights the terrier's predator instinct and its ability to adapt to such a diverse and challenging environment.

In rock den
(Parson Russell Terrier - Mambo's Gunner)

Every natural den presents unique challenges, making each terrier's work an exceptional experience. It might face narrow tunnels, unexpected obstacles like roots or rocks, or have to cross muddy or unstable sections. The terrier is not intimidated by these difficulties; instead, it faces them with determination and agility, demonstrating great problem-solving ability.

It must quickly assess the conditions inside the den, adapt to various situations, and make instinctive decisions to reach its goal. Its intelligence combined with its hunting instinct enables it to effectively tackle the challenges that arise along the way.

Furthermore, working in the natural den creates a strong bond between the dog and its handler. Mutual trust, nonverbal communication, and cooperation are crucial to the success of this activity. The handler must interpret the terrier's signals and guide it safely. Once the terrier enters the den, it becomes independent and must rely on its own abilities to handle the situation.

We cannot overlook the importance of the terrier's safety during work in the natural den. Trainers and handlers take precautionary measures to protect the dog from potential dangers like unstable tunnels, fierce animals, or hidden traps. The priority is always to ensure the dog's safety and well-being throughout the operation.

Once again, the terrier demonstrates its versatility and dedication in performing assigned tasks, offering invaluable assistance to humans in their endeavors. It's an engaging experience that represents not only a way to preserve and enhance the dog's innate abilities but also a special bond between humans and their loyal companion in the pursuit of challenge and adventure in the natural den.

The most famous Russell Terriers

Trump is a Russell Terrier that gained great fame as the founder of the Jack and Parson Russell Terrier breeds. But equally famous in hunting, just like Trump, is the favorite dog of John Russell, "Tip".

Trump

We like to think that its story has become legendary due to its extraordinary abilities and bold character, even though details of its life don't come to us. What may have made Tip so famous was his unique talent for hunting foxes in the English countryside. He could instinctively follow the signals left by his terrier predecessors, like the scent left by foxes or the tracks left in the burrows. As Tip approached the den, his excitement grew, and his energy became overwhelming. He could dig with incredible speed and ferocity, breaking through the tough terrain to reach his prey. His hunting instinct was honed and precise, allowing him to locate foxes even in the most intricate dens.

But what truly set him apart was his ability to confront foxes once he reached them. Despite his smaller size compared to his prey, Tip wasn't intimidated. He faced foxes with courage and tenacity, putting his own safety on the line to protect his territory and complete the hunt.

Tip fascinated and inspired numerous hunting enthusiasts and lovers of Russell Terriers. Despite the lack of information about his true story, we love to remember him as John Russell's favorite, imagining his daring feats and tireless spirit.

It's interesting to note the connection between Carlisle Tack and the terriers of The Parson (Jack) John Russell.

Carlisle Tack

Carlisle Tack was likely a terrier derived from the terriers of the Reverend John Russell, and the fact that it was developed in 1883, the year of John Russell's death, adds another element of historical relevance.

The Reverend Russell's desire to have terriers large enough to run with horses and hunting dogs reflects his passion for hunting. The terriers of the Rev. Russell became known for their abilities in fox hunting; their courage, determination, and compact size made them ideal for chasing prey through underground terrain and across the countryside.

The history and legacy of Russell and his terriers have had a significant impact on the bloodlines of Carlisle Tack and other terrier breeds developed later. The Reverend's passion for hunting and his dedication to breeding terriers suitable for this activity contributed to creating extraordinary dogs that became renowned for their working abilities in burrows and their bold character.

Old Jock was a famous Fox Terrier who lived in the 19th century, from 1859 to 1871. He was predominantly white and gained fame during the late 19th century for his victories in dog shows.

Initially, Old Jock was part of a kennel, where he spent a brief period as a hunting dog. However, his potential as a show dog was later discovered. He participated in numerous dog competitions, showcasing his elegance, proud bearing, and abilities.

His greatest triumph occurred at a dog show that helped popularize the Fox Terrier breed. From then on, Old Jock became a true celebrity in the canine world, admired for his beauty and charming temperament.

Old Jock (on the left), Grove Nettle e Tartar,

One of Old Jock's most famous rivalries was with another dog named Tartar. Both were prominent representatives of the Fox Terrier breed in shows, and their intense competition drew public attention.

In addition to being a well-known Fox Terrier, Old Jock had a significant impact on the Russell Terrier and Dandie Dinmont Terrier breeds. His lineage and contribution to breeding were relevant to the development and preservation of these two breeds.

Despite his short life, Old Jock left a lasting legacy in the world of dog shows and cynology in general. Even today, his name is remembered and honored by dog enthusiasts and breeders, acknowledging his role in elevating the popularity and reputation of the Fox Terrier as a breed.

Barney is a renowned Jack Russell of Arthur Heinemann who has left an indelible mark in the world of burrowing work. His name has become synonymous with skill, intelligence, and tireless dedication to hunting.

From the beginning of his life, Barney showed an extraordinary passion for tracking prey and discovering underground burrows. Even as a puppy, his innate instinct to follow tracks and utilize his digging abilities was evident.

Barney developed an exceptional ability to detect and follow badger tracks. He could pick up the subtlest scent nuances and identify signals left by other terriers that had traversed the territory before him.

His digging prowess was unparalleled. Barney could transform hard and compact terrain into an intricate labyrinth of tunnels with astonishing ease. His digging technique was meticulous and swift, allowing him to reach the badger's burrow in record time.

Once at the burrow, Barney displayed remarkable courage and determination. Despite the potential challenges and difficulties he might encounter within the burrows, he didn't back down. He confronted badgers with a combination of cunning and fierceness, using all his resources to successfully complete the hunt.

His ability to adapt to different situations was impressive. Regardless of the terrain or environmental conditions, Barney always found a way to overcome obstacles and reach his goal. His agility and quick thinking made him an exceptional terrier in burrowing work.

Sportsman, Huntsman and Terriermen

In the captivating context of fox hunting in the 19th century, the distinct roles of the Sportsman, Huntsman, and Terrierman would play a significant part during the thrilling hunting outings, providing rural aristocracy with an unforgettable experience.

The Sportsmen represented adventurous and passionate individuals. Fox hunting was considered one of the most prestigious and refined sports of the era, and Sportsmen participated with enthusiasm and determination. They were often recognizable by their traditional hunting attire and their tendency to follow the hunt on horseback. Their participation in the hunt was typically seen as a symbol of social status and belonging to a certain class. Elegantly mounted on their horses and accompanied by fellow noble hunters, they ventured into the English countryside in search of exciting adventures.

The Huntsmen were usually individuals from privileged social classes, often coming from nobility or affluent bourgeoisie. They engaged in fox hunting as a recreational and entertainment activity, pursuing it for the pleasure and excitement it offered. The Huntsman held a significant role during fox hunting. Adept in hunting and knowledgeable about fox habits, they skillfully led the team of hunters and hunting dogs. With a whistle or melodious signal, they initiated the pursuit of the fox, guiding the hunters in an exhilarating horseback chase. Their ability to track the fox's trail and their guidance created a harmonious interaction between men, horses, and hunting dogs, making fox hunting an engaging and passionate experience.

The Terrierman brought expertise and courage to the group. On the other hand, terriermen were specialized figures dedicated to the technical and practical aspects of fox hunting. Their primary role was to work with terriers, dogs specifically trained to enter fox dens and confront them. Terriermen were true experts in identifying and locating fox dens, thanks to their deep knowledge of these animals' habits and behavior. This skill enabled them to meticulously prepare and position the nets used to trap the foxes during the bolting phase.

The Terrierman was essential when the fox sought refuge underground to escape pursuit. With the help of brave terriers, trained specifically for this task, they endeavored to flush out the fox. The terriers' barking marked the beginning of an exciting challenge between the fox and the courageous dogs beneath the ground.

While sportsmen participated in hunting for fun and sporting challenge, terriermen were crucial for the success and safety of the hunting expeditions. Their experience and skill in working with terriers were essential to ensure that foxes were confronted and captured safely. Terriermen were also responsible for managing the nets and equipment necessary for fox trapping, working closely with sportsmen to coordinate the entire hunting operation.

In an era when fox hunting represented an elegant display of skill and prestige, Sportsmen, Huntsmen, and Terriermen came together in perfect harmony of experience and passion. Guided by their connection with nature and a passion for adventure, they created indelible memories of excitement and fulfillment amid the splendid expanses of the English countryside.

The Last Terriermen

The last terriermen are legendary figures who have played a vital role in rural traditions for centuries. Originally employed to control populations of foxes and badgers that posed a threat to agricultural properties, terriermen were experts in tracking the dens of wild animals and used terrier dogs to flush them out. Over time, their role has evolved, focusing more on wildlife conservation and sustainable species management.

Their expertise in recognizing and managing animal dens provides crucial information about wildlife populations and territories. Collaborating with conservation organizations and agencies, they actively contribute to monitoring and protecting natural habitats. Additionally, they participate in the rehabilitation of injured or needy wild animals, working alongside animal protection associations.

However, the role of terriermen goes beyond wildlife conservation. They also play a significant role in passing down rural traditions to new generations. Through events, demonstrations, and teaching traditional techniques such as working with terrier dogs and identifying dens, they preserve ancient wildlife management practices and keep alive the cultural roots of rural communities.

Nevertheless, terriermen face challenges and controversies related to hunting and wildlife management. Hunting laws have been subject to debate and changes over the years, and there may be restrictions that limit terriermen's activities. Conflicting opinions exist about the ethics of hunting and its compatibility with wildlife conservation. These complex challenges require finding a balance between preserving traditions and respecting contemporary laws and ethical norms.

It's also important to acknowledge the huntsmen and sportsmen who have contributed to and developed teaching methods and have been dedicated to dog selection. Fox hunting has gone beyond the hunting aspect, becoming a symbol of culture and tradition, a deep connection with nature, and a way to pass down hunting skills, courage, and loyalty from generation to generation.

Charles James Apperley, also known as Nimrod, was a passionate English sportsman and writer who left an indelible mark on the history of fox hunting. Born in 1775 and passing away in 1843, he is universally recognized as the father of fox hunting due to his in-depth knowledge and love for this sport.

Through his writing, Apperley shared his passion for fox hunting, publishing several books that have become landmarks for enthusiasts. Among his most famous works are "Nimrod's Hunting Tour" from 1835 and "The Life of a Sportsman" from 1842. In these works, he narrated his adventures, providing detailed descriptions of his hunting experiences, techniques, and traditions associated with fox hunting.

Apperley's works were not just accounts of his personal exploits but also important contributions to fox hunting literature. His engaging and passionate writing conveyed the very essence of the sport, capturing readers' imaginations and spreading knowledge and appreciation for hunting.

Nimrod was not only a talented writer but also a skilled and experienced hunter. His deep understanding of hunting techniques and his ability to work in harmony with foxhounds made him a respected figure in the fox hunting community.

Charles James Apperley's legacy in fox hunting is of fundamental importance. His writing contributed to spreading knowledge and appreciation for the sport, inspiring generations of subsequent hunters. He is remembered as one of the great pioneers of fox hunting, and his impact on hunting culture continues to be recognized to this day.

John Peel was a renowned English huntsman known for his exceptional skill in training and managing Foxhounds. Born in 1776 and passing away in 1854, his influence and expertise have left a lasting mark on the history of fox hunting.

Peel spent over 40 years as a huntsman with the Duke of Beaufort's Hunt, one of England's most prestigious and ancient hunting associations. During his lengthy tenure, he significantly contributed to the development and refinement of the modern Foxhound, the breed of dogs specifically trained for fox hunting.

Peel's dedication and passion in training and leading his Foxhounds were admired by many hunting enthusiasts. His ability to conduct hunting expeditions and manage the hounds contributed to the success of his hunting endeavors and the reputation of the Duke of Beaufort's Hunt.

His influence extended beyond the realm of fox hunting. Peel was a beloved and respected figure in the local community, admired not only for his hunting skills but also for his affable personality and generous spirit. His memory has remained alive in local traditions and popular culture,

to the extent that he became the subject of a famous folk song titled "D'ye ken John Peel?"
John Peel is remembered as an iconic figure of fox hunting, a master in training and managing Foxhounds, and a highly skilled hunter. His legacy lives on through his influence in the world of hunting and in the hearts of those who admire his contributions to the sport.

John Russell, also known as "The Sporting Parson", was an English terrierman who left a significant mark on the history of terriers. Born in 1795 and passing away in 1883, Russell embodied a dual identity: on one hand, he was a respected clergyman of the Church, and on the other, a passionate hunter and terrier breeder. His influence in selecting and developing working dogs was pivotal, particularly in creating the renowned terrier breed known today as the Parson Russell Terrier and Jack Russell Terrier.
He devoted much of his life to fox hunting, considering it not only a sport but also a form of population control for foxes harmful to agriculture. He believed that to achieve the best results in fox hunting, high-quality terriers suitable for fieldwork were necessary. Thus, he began selecting and crossing dogs that possessed the ideal hunting characteristics, such as courage, agility, endurance, and a strong prey drive.
His commitment to terrier selection focused on obtaining dogs capable of following foxes underground and bolting them from their dens. He was particularly attentive to ensuring that the dogs had a suitable physical conformation for agile movement in tunnels and the right combination of intelligence and determination to confront the fox.

Russell was known for his attention to detail and dedication to selective breeding. He did not settle for mediocre dogs but constantly sought to improve the breed and preserve its distinctive qualities. He was selective in choosing pairings and tested his dogs'

hunting abilities before using them for breeding. This rigorous selection process led to the creation of a line of exceptional terriers that carry his name, the Jack Russell Terrier and the Parson Russell Terrier.

Thanks to his work, the Russell Terrier became known for its liveliness, intelligence, and tireless energy. It was a versatile dog, capable of tackling a variety of tasks in hunting, including flushing and bolting foxes, as well as hunting other small animals like rabbits and badgers. It was a loyal companion to hunters and an affectionate friend to families who appreciated its spirited personality and adventurous spirit.

During his lifetime, he bred several successful hunting dogs. Among his most famous hunting dogs are:

Trump, considered the founder of the Russell Terrier breed. He was a sturdy, agile, and courageous terrier known for his excellent digging ability and prowess in fox hunting.

In addition to his influence in terrier selection, Russell was also a respected figure for his knowledge and experience in fox hunting. He was a master in handling dogs during hunts and had an in-depth understanding of fox habits and behavior. He was a mentor to many young terriermen who sought to learn from him the techniques and strategies for successful hunting.

Russell worked closely with the Duke of Beaufort's Hunt, providing his terrierman services for fox hunting. His extensive knowledge of foxes and terriers was widely respected, and his hunting skills were considered essential for the success of hunting expeditions. Russell's reputation quickly grew, and his passion for terriers and fox hunting became infectious.

He was highly sought after as a judge in dog shows, where he evaluated both the conformation and working qualities of terriers. His experience and in-depth knowledge of the breed granted him great authority and respect in the field. The figure of John Russell has remained an icon in the world of terriers and fox hunting. His contribution to creating the Russell Terrier and improving the breed has had a lasting impact, so much so that the name John Russell is closely linked to the breed to this day. His dedication and commitment to terrier work laid the foundation for the high popularity and appreciation of these dogs by hunters and animal lovers worldwide.

Today, the Jack and Parson Russell Terrier are admired for their liveliness, indomitable spirit, and intelligence. They continue to be cherished as working dogs for their ability to hunt and track foxes, as well as beloved pets for their loyalty and spirited personality. John Russell's legacy lives on through this wonderful terrier breed, carrying forward his passion for hunting and love for adventure.

George Osbaldeston was a renowned English sportsman whose fox hunting prowess set numerous records. Born in 1786 and passing away in 1866, his extraordinary hunting career made him a legendary figure in the world of fox hunting. Osbaldeston is primarily known for his remarkable number of foxes captured during his lifetime. It is estimated that he hunted and captured over 2,000 foxes, an extraordinary achievement that attests to his dedication and talent in hunting. His skill and reputation as a fox hunter made him a figure of great admiration in the hunting community. His successes became legendary and inspired many subsequent hunters to emulate him. He was not only a highly skilled hunter but also a passionate advocate for fox hunting as a sport. His passion for hunting and his dedication to promoting and preserving this tradition became an integral part of his legacy. George Osbaldeston is remembered as one of the greatest fox hunters of his time, whose name is synonymous with skill, success, and dedication to fox hunting.

Richard Ansdell was born in 1815 in Liverpool, England. He demonstrated artistic talent from a young age and pursued artistic studies at the prestigious Royal Academy of Arts in London. It was in the 1840s that he began to focus on painting animal subjects, particularly terriers. Richard Ansdell's terrier paintings became highly popular and contributed to solidifying his reputation as one of the most important terrier painters in art history. His works capture the energy, vitality, and distinctive nature of these fascinating canine breeds. With great skill and mastery, Ansdell portrayed terriers in various situations and settings, capturing their determination, courage, and intelligence. His paintings are known for the liveliness of the dogs' expressions, attention to anatomical details, and realistic rendering of fur and coat. Richard Ansdell's fame as a terrier painter spread rapidly, earning him a following of admirers and collectors. His works were exhibited in major art shows and garnered recognition and awards. His technical ability and precision in representing terriers helped define the standards of representation for these breeds in painting. Some of his most famous terrier-centered works include: "A Young girl with a Terrier" - This painting depicts a terrier alongside a girl, emphasizing the close bond between the dog and its young companion. "A Terrier win a Rabbit" - In this scene, a terrier is depicted with a rabbit in its mouth, the spoils of the hunt. His skill in portraying these animals, along with his mastery in capturing action and expression, made him one of the most celebrated terrier painters of his time. In addition to terriers, Ansdell also painted other animal subjects, such as horses, cattle, and wildlife. His artistic career was long and fruitful, and his works are still appreciated and admired today. Richard Ansdell left a lasting imprint on the art world, thanks to his mastery in portraying terriers and his ability to capture the essence of canine breeds. His paintings remain a testament to his talent and his passion for the animal world, influencing generations of subsequent artists and continuing to evoke admiration among art and animal lovers.

Joe Bowman, born in 1857 in the Lake District, England, was a prominent figure in the world of hunting and breeding Patterdale Terriers. He is widely recognized for his contribution to the development of the breed and bringing it to its current form. From a young age, he displayed an innate passion for hunting dogs, particularly terriers. With determination and dedication, he devoted much of his life to breeding and selecting Patterdale Terriers, tirelessly working to improve the breed's characteristics. Bowman's reputation as a terrierman was well-established and recognized in the hunting community. He was known for his skill in training and working with terriers. His in-depth knowledge of canine behavior, combined with extensive field experience, allowed him to achieve exceptional performances from his hunting dogs. Bowman passed on his passion and experience to other hunters and terrier enthusiasts. He was a respected and admired figure in the terrierman community, always ready to share his knowledge and offer advice on training and terrier management. In addition to his hunting and breeding activities, Joe Bowman was also an advocate for responsible and sustainable hunting. He emphasized the importance of respecting laws and conservation regulations, ensuring the survival of wildlife species and the preservation of natural habitats. His passion for Patterdale Terriers and hunting has endured over time, influencing the terrierman community and contributing to the preservation of the terrier hunting tradition. His legacy is evident today, with Patterdale Terriers representing a revered and appreciated breed known for their hunting abilities and tenacious nature. Joe Bowman, a man dedicated to his passion for terriers and hunting, left a significant mark in the history of canine breeds and hunting culture. His skill in working with terriers and his contribution to breed development stand as a testament to his commitment and determination to preserve the traditions and skills of terriermen.

Arthur Heinemann was a well-known British terrierman in the world of terrier hunting. Born in 1927, Heinemann became a prominent figure in earthwork hunting thanks to his extraordinary skills in handling working dogs and his passion for hunting. Heinemann began his career at a young age, following in the footsteps of his father, who was also an experienced terrierman. Over the years, Heinemann honed his terrier hunting skills and developed a deep bond with his dogs. One of his most famous and beloved dogs was Brock, an exceptional and courageous Jack Russell Terrier. Brock became an icon in the world of terrier hunting due to his incredible fox-catching abilities and his indomitable spirit. Heinemann was known for his ability to guide his dogs underground during hunts, working in perfect harmony with them to locate and hunt prey. He was a highly respected terrierman admired for his dedication to hunting and the care and attention he devoted to his dogs. In addition to hunting, Heinemann was also a prolific writer, authoring numerous books and articles on terrier hunting and working dog management. His works helped spread his knowledge and experience in the hunting world and inspired many terrier enthusiasts worldwide. Arthur Heinemann was a reference in the world of terrier hunting, and his contribution to the sector was of fundamental importance. His passion, dedication, and hunting skills inspired and influenced many subsequent terriermen, ensuring that his memory and impact have endured over time.

Brian Plummer was a famous English terrierman and writer, known for his deep knowledge and passion for terriers and earthwork hunting. Born in 1932, Plummer spent much of his life working with hunting dogs, becoming a prominent figure in the world of terrier hunting. From a young age, Brian Plummer developed a strong affinity for dogs, particularly terriers. His skill in training and handling dogs was extraordinary, and he soon became a highly respected and sought-after terrierman. Plummer wrote several books on the subject, with a particular focus on terrier hunting and training. His writings became true "bibles" for terrier enthusiasts, providing valuable information and tips on how to train and manage dogs during underground hunting. In addition to being a prolific writer, Brian Plummer played an important role in organizing events and competitions related to terrier hunting. He contributed to promoting the conservation of terrier breeds and preserving the traditions of this form of hunting. His experience and talent in working with dogs earned him a great reputation, and many people turned to him for consultations and advice on terrier hunting. His ethical and respectful approach to animals made him a respected figure even among those who did not practice hunting. Brian Plummer passed away in 2003, but his legacy in the world of terrier hunting lives on through his writings and his influence on generations of hunters and dog lovers. His dedication to terrier breed conservation and the promotion of ethical practices in hunting left a lasting imprint on the terrierman community and beyond.

David Hancock is a well-known terrierman, writer, and canine scholar. He was born in England in 1944 and is considered an expert on many dog breeds, particularly working terriers. David Hancock has dedicated much of his life to studying and promoting terrier breeds and their traditional use as hunting dogs. He conducted in-depth research into the history and origins of various terrier breeds, contributing to the preservation of hunting traditions and the working characteristics of these breeds. He is the author of numerous books and articles on canines and terrier hunting, significantly contributing to the dissemination of accurate and detailed information about these breeds. His writings reflect his passion and dedication to working dogs and his deep knowledge of canine breed history. David Hancock is also an advocate for ethics in hunting and is committed to promoting responsible and respectful hunting practices toward animals. His work has had a significant impact on the terrierman and hunting dog lover community, and his commitment to preserving hunting traditions and terrier breeds has earned him respect in the canine world.

Bert Gripton is one of the few legendary terrierists known not for breeding dogs, but for their work. He had a small pack of working terriers and whippets and was considered a terrierist for the fox hunters of Albrighton. His father was a gamekeeper on the Aqualate estate in Staffordshire, near the Shropshire border. Gripton was a passionate digger specialized in badger hunting, but he also hunted otters (catching the last legal otter in the UK) and foxes. Phil Drabble, author of "Of Pedigree Unknown: Sporting and Working Dogs", stated that Gripton "could, and did, catch foxes with more certainty than hounds". Bert Gripton seemed to keep a very small pack of dogs. This is not surprising: the more people dig, the more they seem to appreciate a small dog capable of getting close to the prey and maneuvering around it. Brian Nuttall notes that Gripton's terriers were called "white hunt terriers" in those days; no one called them Jack Russells. Phil Drabble explained Gripton's technique for removing a fox: The most frequent image was that of a smiling fox, and in this case, there was an effective trick that required great confidence and dexterity akin to sleight of hand. He would take a piece of wood, as wide as his thumb and about a foot long, and move it quickly across the fox's muzzle, keeping it within reach of its jaws. The fox's reaction was instant: it would bite the stick with a firm grip. At that precise moment, it was the right time to shoot his other hand and grab it by the scruff of the neck. This technique required exceptional calm, more than I possessed, but it was one of Bert Gripton's finest skills.

Alistair Robinson was born in Cumbria, England, in 1964. He began working as a terrierman in the early 1990s and worked for the Ullswater Foxhounds for over 10 years. He gained notoriety in 2009 when he was caught on video digging a fox out of its den and bludgeoning it to death. This episode sparked much controversy and publicity surrounding the use of terriermen in fox hunting. Robinson was convicted of animal cruelty and banned from working with dogs for life. Alistair Robinson was a terrierman born in Cumbria, England, in 1964. He pursued a career as a terrierman in the early 1990s and was employed by the Ullswater Foxhounds for over 10 years. His career was marked by a controversial and dramatic event that garnered attention to terriermen and the practice of fox hunting. In 2009, Alistair Robinson was captured on video digging out an underground fox den and subsequently beating the fox to death. This incident sparked considerable debate and brought public attention to the brutality of acts carried out by terriermen during fox hunting. The incident led to a debate on the ethics and legality of employing terriermen in fox hunting. As a consequence of his actions, Alistair Robinson was convicted of animal cruelty and permanently banned from working with dogs. His actions were deemed not only a violation of animal protection laws but also an abuse of the involved wildlife. The episode involving Alistair Robinson contributed to raising public awareness about ethical issues and the regulation of fox hunting in the UK. It became a landmark case in the debate between supporters and opponents of fox hunting and contributed to advancing the idea of stricter legislation to ensure the welfare of animals involved in such hunting practices.

Eddie Chapman, born in 1943 and recently passed away, was a respected and esteemed figure in the world of

Russell Terriers. Regarded as one of the top professional terrier experts in the United Kingdom, his passion for these dogs began when, as a young boy, he was engaged in shooting rats at a dump. It was during one of these occasions that he encountered an elderly man accompanied by several terriers, busy hunting and killing rats amidst the garbage. This chance encounter marked a turning point in Eddie's life as he developed a deep passion for these dogs.

This man, nicknamed Knocker, was a Russell Terrier enthusiast, and his extensive knowledge of their behavior and skills made them effective even in challenging situations like unstable slopes, cliffs, quarries, and old mines where local foxes often sought refuge. Thanks to a combination of instinct and the Russell Terriers' abilities, Knocker achieved remarkable hunting results.

Eddie Chapman was also influenced by other key individuals like Charles Parker and Gerald Jones, who helped him further develop his knowledge of the breed. Particularly, Gerald Jones shared with him his love for Russell Terriers and the history of their founder, John Russell. Mr. Jones' house was a sort of museum dedicated to John Russell, but unfortunately, it was destroyed by fire.

Another significant moment in Eddie's life was when he participated in a show with his dog Sinbad, and the Duke of Beaufort showed great interest in his specimen, recognizing the importance of terrier bloodlines. For Eddie, preserving the purity of Russell Terrier bloodlines was paramount, so he consistently dedicated himself to researching the best available lines, focusing on eight distinct lines for breeding.

Eddie Chapman's evident satisfaction lies in the fact that the terriers he bred are still highly regarded for their beauty, exceptional temperament, and intelligence. He proudly shares the positive experiences of lucky Foxwarren terrier owners, who consider these dogs an integral part of the family and special companions.

After fifty years of dedication to breeding at Foxwarren, Eddie Chapman finds contentment in the results achieved with his terriers, which continue to be recognized for their authenticity and unique character. His policy of preserving the original bloodlines has borne fruit, as the terriers he breeds today remain true to the Russell Terrier tradition. The strict preservation of bloodlines ensured that the dogs maintained their excellence in work and stood out for their distinct intelligence and temperament.

In addition to his passion for the breed, Eddie Chapman has always cared about spreading the true Russell Terrier, lending his dogs to other hunters who didn't have the opportunity to initiate a large breeding program. This gesture allowed other people to experience the joy of working with an authentic Russell Terrier.

For Eddie Chapman, the preservation of the true Russell Terrier was a significant mission in his life. His experiences, attention to detail, and dedication to bloodline work enabled him to create a lineage of terriers that faithfully embodies the spirit and characteristics of the breed.

An Imaginary Hunting Expedition

On a crisp morning in the picturesque landscape of 19th-century rural England, Reverend John Russell, a man of devout heart and a passion for hunting, was getting ready for a day of thrilling adventure. He wore his clergy robe, but over it, he donned a stylish hunting jacket, ready to unite his faith and passion in a singular purpose.

Beside him stood a few nobles, Lord Edward Beaumont and Lady Margaret Fairchild, avid hunters and great admirers of Reverend Russell. They had heard of his fox hunting skills and insisted he join them for an unforgettable hunting day.

The trio was accompanied by a group of skilled terriermen, led by Charles Bennett, renowned for his knowledge of dens and his skill in working with terrier dogs. Bennett was respected by both the nobility and Reverend Russell for his integrity and passion for dogs.

As the unmistakable sound of the hunting horn signaled the start of the hunting expedition, the team set off across green meadows and stretches of woods, while the Foxhounds brimmed with excitement, sniffing the air for fox tracks. It was a moment of joy and adventure, where the sound of horse hooves and the barking of dogs blended with the surrounding nature.

After a while, the dogs picked up the fresh trail of a fox, and the chase began. Reverend Russell proved himself a skilled hunter, leading the group with wisdom and courage. Lord Edward and Lady Margaret rode alongside him, brimming with enthusiasm and ready to seize every opportunity for a sure shot.

The terriermen followed closely, prepared to intervene when the fox took refuge in a den. With skill and precision, Bennett guided the terriers to the den, encouraging them to work in synergy to flush out the fox from its hiding place.

It was a sequence of moments of tension and joy as the fox desperately tried to elude the eager hunting party. Reverend Russell, despite his religious calling, exhibited an unmatched passion and determination, showing that hunting and faith could coexist in perfect harmony.

The hunt commenced, and the nobles and men dispersed in different directions, hoping to catch a glimpse of the elusive prey. The fox, in a cunning maneuver, darted into a intricate labyrinth of underground dens, trying to disorient the pursuing dogs.

Max, a courageous terrier, with his keen nose and unwavering determination, began to follow the scent trail of the fox. The dens twisted and forked, but Max seemed to have an innate understanding of which direction to take. Deep within the den, the fox sensed the looming presence of the terrier on its tail. Tension hung thick as the hunt continued.

Russell, with his experience, realized that the fox was attempting to lead the terrier into a dead-end, but Max, emboldened by his experience, slowed his pace and carefully assessed the arrangement of tunnels. And so, the fox and Max found themselves in a kind of dance within the den, a ballet of intuition and cunning. There was no physical contact, but a fascinating battle of wills and wit. The fox sought to bewilder Max, but the brave terrier wasn't fooled. With agile and swift movements, the fox tried to shake off Max amidst the intricate underground passages, but the terrier remained steadfast in his pursuit.

As Max continued to follow the fox through the intricate underground passages, an unusual sensation swept over him. He felt a slight tremor coming from the ground and a deep sound of cracking. The terrier perked up his ears and sniffed the air, sensing a change in the atmosphere. His instincts told him that something was about to happen. Suddenly, a rumble echoed through the den. A tunnel collapsed, creating an opening in the ground, letting in dust and debris. The fox was trapped, and Max instinctively began to bark. Meanwhile, the terriermen and nobles who remained at the entrance of the den were startled by the sudden collapse, visible to the naked eye. Concerned for Max's safety, they hastened to initiate rescue operations.

The terriermen, identifying the point where Max was barking, began to dig frantically, removing earth and debris to free the brave trapped dog. Finally, after intense digging efforts, the terriermen reached Max and captured the fox. The terrier, exhausted but still determined, emerged from the tunnel with his tail held high and his eyes gleaming with joy. He was free and ready to resume his mission. Despite the collapse of the den causing a momentary pause, the terrier's courage and tenacity hadn't waned. He was ready to continue his work.

The fox was released, and so Max and his fellow terriermen regrouped, ready to continue the fox hunt. The tunnel collapse hadn't stopped their determination, but it had added an element of challenge and adrenaline to their adventure. Over the next few hours, Max would continue to chase the fox with renewed fervor, navigating tight and intricate passages, overcoming obstacles, and getting closer and closer to his elusive target.

The story of that day, with the tunnel collapse and Max's courageous digging, would be passed down through the years as a memorable episode of fox hunting. It would add a captivating chapter to Max's legacy as an extraordinary terrier, willing to overcome the toughest trials to pursue his passion for hunting.

Admiring Max's bravery and skill, Lady Margaret turned to Russell and Bennett, offering them sincere praise for their exceptional work. The hunt was over, but the unforgettable experience would remain etched in the memories of all who had witnessed that battle of intellect and skill. Lord Edward, Lady Margaret, and the terriermen bid each other farewell with respect and gratitude, aware that the day would be forever remembered.

From that moment on, Max and the terriermen would be remembered as the protagonists of one of the most fascinating and unforgettable hunting expeditions of the time, where the wild nature and human ingenuity had merged in an unprecedented ballet.

And so, the story of that day's fox hunt spread, fueling the myth of Max and his legendary courage. The underground den became a sort of sanctuary, a place where tales of adventure and daring were recounted from generation to generation, keeping the memory of that extraordinary moment alive.

The Hunting Parson

There are few testimonies and memories about Reverend John Russell, and we can only imagine the extraordinary adventures he took part in throughout his life. I envision his days spent between the holy church and the forests, seeking thrills and companionship for his dogs.

I picture Russell, with his determined character and passion for hunting, engrossed in his role as a terrierman. I see him walking across the fields, trailed by his faithful terriers, ready to run and unearth game. His imposing figure and determined gaze command respect and admiration.

In his adventures, I see him engaged in battles of wits with foxes. His skill in understanding their movements and predicting their actions makes him a formidable opponent. With his tireless terrier by his side, he ventures into the woods in search of fox tracks, following their distinct scent that electrifies the air.

I imagine the fervor and passion as he watches his terriers spring into action. Their agility and determination in pursuing the fox are captivating to witness. The Reverend, his heart swelling with pride, encourages his dogs, knowing that their success hinges on their synergy and innate instinct.

And on those rare occasions when the fox manages to elude capture, I see him welcoming it as a triumph of the animal's cunning and intelligence. Despite the disappointment of a missed catch, Reverend Russell appreciates the beauty and majesty of the wilderness.

His adventures remind us that hunting is not just about prey and conquest, but also about respect for animals and the environment that surrounds us. His passion for terriers and hunting reflects his deep connection with nature and his dedication to preserving the beauty and balance of the ecosystem.

And so, even though the stories and memories of the Reverend may seem shrouded in mystery and legend, we know that his impact on the world of terriers and hunting has been profound. His legacy lives on through the terrier dogs that bear his name and through the inspiration he still ignites in the hearts of those who love nature and adventure.

Reverend John Russell, the devoted terrierman and man of faith, is a symbol of passion, courage, and respect for wildlife. His tales urge us to explore our relationship with the natural world and to recognize the intrinsic beauty of life and the environment around us. He teaches us that hunting is not merely a quest for thrills or trophies, but a way to connect with nature and appreciate the complexity and balance of ecosystems.

In his vision, the terrier is the true protagonist of these adventures. Not just a hunting companion, but an animal endowed with intelligence, bravery, and extraordinary determination. The terrier embodies the very essence of hunting, with its ability to unearth, chase, and confront prey with an indomitable passion.

He has left an indelible mark on terrier history, with his dedication to preserving the characteristics and qualities that make these dogs so special. His attention to careful selection and care in the breeding and training of terriers has helped keep alive the traditions and values that accompany this age-old hunting practice.

But his legacy extends beyond the world of terriers. Reverend Russell reminds us of the importance of respecting and protecting nature. His stories invite us to explore and live in harmony with the environment that surrounds us, to appreciate the beauty and diversity of the species that inhabit the earth.

Today, terriers continue to play a significant role in hunting activities, but they are also beloved as family companions and affectionate pets. Their energy, indomitable spirit, and loyalty are admired by many, much like Reverend John Russell admired them.

Whether it's a fox hunt, a stroll in the woods, or moments of play in the backyard, terriers accompany us with their contagious enthusiasm and unconditional loyalty. They are the true protagonists of our story, teaching us the importance of fully embracing each moment and cherishing the deep bond we share with animals and the natural world.

Thus, as we conclude this journey into the world of terriers and hunting, let us always remember Reverend John Russell and his extraordinary contribution. His love for terriers and his dedication to preserving hunting traditions inspire us to cultivate a deeper connection with nature and appreciate the fundamental role animals play in our world. Whether in the pursuit of the fox or in the simple company of a faithful terrier, let us celebrate the unique bond between humans and dogs, bearing witness to the timeless value of this ancient practice and the legacy left behind by Reverend John Russell, the terrierman who made terriers the true protagonists of our adventures in nature.

Conclusions

And so, with these pages filled with adventures, we come to the conclusion of this book dedicated to terriers. Through these words, we have explored the historical roots of this captivating breed and delved into their world of work and dedication.

We have discovered how terriers have been tireless companions of terriermen, hunters, and nobles, standing by their side in their challenges and adventures in the English countryside. They have been the true silent heroes, always ready to showcase their skill and intuition for fox, badger, or other subterranean prey hunting.

Throughout the pages of this book, we have seen how the terrier is much more than just a companion dog or a show dog. It is an indefatigable worker, an animal that gives its all to achieve its set goals. Its strength, courage, and tenacity have been highlighted in every anecdote, every story, and every image we've explored, always in the spirit of providing valuable insight without delving too deeply into the topics. Many such writings would be needed to describe the countless deeds of the protagonists and to delve deeper into the world of their work and its countless techniques.

But as we reflect on their tireless work and their contribution to hunting, we must remind ourselves that the terrier is the true protagonist of this story. It is the one who, with its daring and skill, has brought light and success to every hunting adventure. It is the one who has proven to be a loyal and faithful companion, ready to sacrifice itself to serve its master. We must pay homage to all the terriers who have been integral parts of these pages, to those who have trodden the English lands.

We can appreciate their courage, their intelligence, and their passion for the work they do. We can learn from their dedication and loyalty, remembering that terriers are more than just hunting dogs: they are true heroes deserving of our respect and admiration.

May these words and stories continue to resonate in the hearts of those who love terriers and may they continue to spread awareness of their unique and special role in the world of hunting and beyond. Whether in the green fields of England or in distant lands, terriers will continue to carry out their work with the same passion and determination as ever. We can be grateful for their innate instinct, their ability to unearth and pursue the wild, and the joy they bring us when we see them in action.

But beyond their role in hunting, terriers also teach us important life lessons. They show us the importance of perseverance, tenacity, and loyalty. They remind us that even in the face of adversity, we can tackle challenges with courage and determination.

So, as we close this book, let us never forget the importance of terriers in preserving ancient traditions. Because, in the end, the terrier is the true protagonist of this story. And it will always be so, in every hunting expedition, in every dug-out burrow, and in every heart that has been won over by their courage and tenacity.

Dear terriers, thank you for all that you are.

Printed in Great Britain
by Amazon

33034888R00096